STUDENT

HACKS

STUDENT ESSENTIALS FOR UNIVERSITY: THE MODERN UNI HANDBOOK WITH CUTTING-EDGE STRATEGIES AND TIPS FOR TODAY'S ACADEMIC JOURNEY

BEN STEPHENS

TABLE OF CONTENTS

ALRIGHT, YOU LOVELY LOT!

Pull up a chair, pop the kettle on, and lend an ear. Yours truly here was once just like you – shuffling between lectures, burning toast in shared kitchens, and frantically Googling "how to adult". Survived it, got the degree and the ever-so-slightly overused student mug to prove it.

Now, why did I scribble down this book, you ask? Because there's a shitload of advice out there, but let's be honest, most of it's pure waffle. This ain't your typical book, written by a team of suits in a swanky office block. No, mate. I've had chinwags with hundreds of uni students from Land's End to John O'Groats, and they've spilled the beans on the real McCoy – hacks that genuinely work.

In short? This book wipes away the codswallop and cuts straight to the chase. No faffing about. Just straight-up, tried-and-true wisdom without making your head spin.

So, if you fancy a no-nonsense guide that's as straight-up as a pint in your local, you're in the right place. Cheers to smarter, not harder, student life!

THE LAY OF THE LAND

Tech and Digital Tools for learning: Tired of the spinning wheel of doom or apps that promise the moon but deliver a pebble? We've sifted through the digital noise to bring you the crème de la crème of tech tools, guaranteed to make your life a smidge easier.

Budgeting and Saving Money: Ah, the classic student dilemma: do I buy that textbook or indulge in a cheeky takeaway? Let's get you squared away with top tips to save those precious quid without compromising on life's little luxuries. Who said beans on toast is all a student can afford?

Time Management: You ever feel like there aren't enough hours in the day, especially when the new series drops on Netflix? Here's how to juggle the jigs and the reels of student life, without missing out on the fun bits.

Study and Revision Hacks: Dive headfirst into the labyrinth of lectures, notes, and all-nighters. Fancy acing that exam without going stark raving mad? Or maybe you just fancy a bit more kip? We've got the tips and tricks to keep you sharp without having you guzzle down your weight in energy drinks.

Social Life and Networking: From making pals that'll last a lifetime to schmoozing at events without breaking a sweat, we'll help you put your best foot forward. No more awkward mingling at parties or missing out on events because you "didn't get the memo."

Health and Wellbeing: Between late-night study sessions and impromptu nights out, it's easy to let yourself go a bit pear-shaped. Discover hacks for keeping both your noggin and your body in tip-top shape, all while enjoying the student life to the max.

Dormitory/Shared Living Hacks: Dive into the beautiful chaos of shared living. From ensuring your milk doesn't mysteriously 'evaporate' to handling the mate who's forgotten what headphones are, we've got you covered. Sharing is caring, but there's a method to the madness.

NOW, BEFORE WE CRACK....

Hold up a sec. I can almost hear you thinking, "Oi, is this one of those sneaky sponsored gigs?" Let me set the record straight. Not a single app, tool, or tip mentioned in this book has slipped us a cheeky tenner to get a mention. No backhanders, no crafty deals. This ain't the Premier League, mate.

Why's that important? 'Cause it means we've got no biases. Everything scribbled down here is the dog's bollocks – tried and tested, no strings attached. The hacks you're about to dive into? Pure, unfiltered wisdom straight from the horse's mouth (well, students' mouths, but you get the gist).

So rest easy. It's just you, me, and a goldmine of student hacks. Let's get stuck in, shall we?

01 Chapter 1 - Tech and Digital Tools for learning

WHY WE'RE KICKING OFF WITH ON STUDY AND REVISION WITH DIGITAL TOOLS

Alright, lend me your lugholes for a mo'. You might be wondering why we're diving straight into the world of tech and digital tools, right? Well, it ain't a random choice, mate. We're not shuffling about in the dusty libraries of the past, still clutching onto overhead projectors and floppy disks. No siree!

See, we're students of the now. Living, breathing, and learning in a digital age where our smartphones are sharper than some lecture hall projectors. Our generation? We're hardwired for this century, not stuck in some black and white flashback. We're agile, adaptable, and ready to embrace every byte and pixel that can give us an edge in our studies. We kick off with tech and digital tools 'cause, let's face it, that's our bread and butter. It's the cornerstone of modern learning, and by mastering it, we're not just keeping up — we're blazing the trail.

So, if you've ever scoffed at your grandad's tales of "back in my day, we had to walk to the library in the snow", this section's for you. We're celebrating the now, the new, and the next in learning. Strap in, and let's turbocharge our uni game!

HACK ONE

Unlock the secret to flawless referencing in minutes, not hours!

You're wrapping up your essay, feeling like a rockstar. But then, it hits you: the dreaded references section. You've got quotes and sources scattered all over, and piecing them together feels like trying to assemble IKEA furniture without the manual. Sound familiar?

THE REAL STORY:

Picture Jamie, a third-year Politics student. In his first year, the bloke would lose more time on referencing than on a night out. He'd often end up with citations resembling a jigsaw puzzle with missing pieces. But one frosty morning, after feedback that looked more like a murder scene with red ink, he vowed, "This is it! I'm turning this ship around."

WHAT THE LECTURERS DON'T TELL YOU ABOUT REFERENCES

Oi, mate! Have you ever noticed how lecturers have a knack for dropping hints about important bits but then gloss over the gritty details? Especially when it comes to referencing. They say it's crucial, and yes, it very much is, but there's more to it than just dodging the plagiarism police.
Turn referencing from a chore into your secret weapon!

Now, here's the thing. When you properly reference, it's not just about playing by the rules; it's about showing your lecturer: "Look, Prof, not only did I listen, but I've gone the extra mile. I'm not just regurgitating info – I'm engaging with it."

References are like the subtle nod to the DJ when your favourite tune comes on. It's recognition, a sign of appreciation, a hint that you're tuned in. And believe you me, lecturers love it when students are on the ball. It's like feeding them a scone with just the right amount of clotted cream and jam. Pure delight.

So, the next time you're pulling an all-nighter, don't just slap on references as an afterthought. Use them as your ace in the hole, a little nudge to the lecturer, signalling that you're not just another face in the crowd. You're the student who pays attention, engages, and deserves every bit of recognition that comes your way.

From Reference Rookie to Citation Champion

A mate introduced him to Zotero and Mendeley. They weren't just tools; they were life-savers. A bit like finding out there's a shortcut through campus you never knew about.

Both Zotero and Mendeley are top-tier tools designed to save your bacon when it comes to referencing. Free to use, they're like a student's dream, ready to help you breeze through your essay without breaking a sweat on the citation front. Here's your quick guide to mastering them

ZOTERO:

Get Started:

- Head to the Zotero website.
- Download and install Zotero for your specific OS.
- Register for a free account.

Collecting References:

- Install the Zotero Connector for your browser. This allows you to save references directly from webpages, databases, and library catalogues.
- As you research, click the Zotero Connector icon in your browser to save the citation.

Organise Your Library:

- Open the Zotero app. Your references appear there.
- Create folders (they call them "collections") for different topics or assignments.

Citing While Writing:

- Install the Zotero Word plugin.
- As you write your essay in Word (or LibreOffice), click the Zotero toolbar to insert citations and even generate bibliographies in your chosen style.

MENDELEY:

Get Started:

- Visit the Mendeley website.
- Download and install the Mendeley Desktop app.
- Sign up for a free account.

• Gathering References:

- Install the Mendeley Web Importer in your browser.
- As you come across papers and articles, use the Web Importer to add them to your Mendeley library.

Organise and Read:

- Within the Mendeley Desktop app, you can create folders, annotate documents, and even highlight essential bits.

Cite As You Write:

- Install the Mendeley Reference Manager Word plugin.
- In Word, use the Mendeley toolbar to insert citations and bibliographies tailored to your preferred referencing style.

WHY IT WORKS:

Referencing isn't just a ritual dance to appease the academic gods. It's your chance to show you've done your homework, that you value the wisdom of others, and that you're savvy enough to give them a tip of the hat. And as our mate Jamie realised, with a bit of order and attention, referencing can be less about avoiding trouble and more about earning brownie points, references properly and effectively could just take your essays to the next level.

HACK TWO

The Digital Blueprint: Mastering Essay Structure

You're faced with a daunting blank document. The cursor flashes, almost taunting you. There's a whirlwind of ideas, but laying them out systematically? Ah, the quintessential essay structuring dilemma.

Dive into Lisa's world, a first-year Literature student at York University. For her, essay crafting felt akin to navigating York's historic labyrinthine alleyways without a map. But one chilly evening, whilst exploring a university chat forum, she stumbled upon a digital revelation.

DECIPHERING THE ART OF STRUCTURE:

York's distinguished tutors consistently emphasise the essence of a robust thesis and a compelling analysis. Yet, they seldom delve deep into the golden thread that seamlessly weaves everything together. An essay is akin to a classic British series - it requires episodes that flow seamlessly, leading to an enthralling finale.

FROM CHAOS TO COHERENCE WITH TECH TOOLS:

Welcome to the 21st century, the digital era! Let's employ technology to achieve that seamless essay structure.

Utilising Trello for Essay Planning

Enter: Trello. Primarily a project management tool but a hidden gem for academic planning.

GETTING STARTED WITH TRELLO FOR ESSAYS:

Craft Your Board:

- Begin with a new board titled after your essay subject.

List Your Way:

- Create columns for every essay segment: Introduction, Main Argument, Counter Argument, Conclusion, and so on.

Detail with Cards:

- For each column, add cards detailing main ideas, supporting evidence, and analysis. The perk? You can directly attach links or documents!

Flex & Flow:

- Rearrange cards as your essay evolves. This dynamic drag-and-drop interface ensures fluidity in your argument.

Collaborative Genius:

- Want feedback? Add a peer to your board, allowing for collaborative brainstorming.

VISUAL STRUCTURING WITH XMIND:

- While Trello excels at linear planning, XMind shines for visual thinkers.
- Begin with your core thesis.
- Branch out to main arguments.
- Further down, create nodes for supporting evidence and annotations.
- Customise with colours and icons to make it truly yours.

WHY IT WORKS:

Trello and XMind, these digital allies, transform the essay structuring process from a challenge to a delight. Lisa's journey from structuring apprehension to becoming a structuring maven at York University is testament to the power of harnessing tech. So the next time the daunting task of essay planning looms, remember: Digital tools are right at your fingertips, ready to guide your narrative seamlessly from start to finish.

HACK THREE

From Prolix to Pristine: Hemingway Editor, Your Essay's Best Friend

There's a little secret every student should know: brilliance isn't just about what you say; it's also about how you say it. Especially when the midnight oil's burning and you're typing up a storm.

THE REAL STORY:

Enter the world of Jodi, a third-year Psychology buff at the University of Lancaster. Jodi, with her expansive thoughts and analytical prowess, often found her essays meandering like a river with numerous tributaries. But everything changed during a serendipitous evening with Hemingway Editor.

LATE NIGHT DISCOVERY:

Picture it. University of Lancaster. Midnight. Jodi, surrounded by a mosaic of textbooks and scribbled notes. Desperate for clarity amidst the academic chaos, she stumbled upon Hemingway Editor. She describes her discovery as "finding a lighthouse in a foggy sea of words."

The Unsung Hero of Essay Clarity

Lecturers often commend expansive research and complex ideas. Yet, beneath the surface, they're yearning for a golden thread of clarity weaving through your essay.

Hemingway Editor became Jodi's secret weapon. Here's how you can unlock its full potential:

DEEP DIVE INTO HEMINGWAY EDITOR:

Immediate Feedback:

- Head to the Hemingway Editor website. It's web-based, so no fuss with installations. Once there, paste in your draft. Watch as the editor works its magic, highlighting sections that need your attention

Colour Codes Galore:

- Hemingway doesn't just point out mistakes; it colour-codes them. Yellow for hard-to-read sentences, red for sentences that are convoluted, purple for words with simpler alternatives, blue for adverbs, and green for passive voice.

Readability Score:

- This isn't just a fancy term. The score helps you gauge your essay's complexity. For academic work, hovering around Grades 8-10 ensures depth without sacrificing clarity.

Tweak and Tune:

- As you refine your essay, the colour-coded highlights change. It's interactive, guiding you towards a polished piece.

Formatting Tools:

- Hemingway Editor isn't just about corrections. It provides basic formatting options – bolding, italics, headers, and bullets. Perfect for structuring your essay highlights.

Direct Web Publishing:

If you're working on a digital piece or blog post for class, Hemingway allows you to publish directly to platforms like WordPress or Medium.

JODI'S PRO TIPS FOR MASTERING HEMINGWAY EDITOR:

- Don't Over-rely: While Hemingway is a gem, remember it's a machine. It won't catch nuances or context-specific intricacies. Use it as a guide, not the definitive authority.
- Practice Makes Perfect: Familiarize yourself with Hemingway by pasting different types of texts. Understand why it makes certain suggestions. Over time, you'll preemptively avoid mistakes before they happen.
- Draft First, Edit Later: Pour out your thoughts first. Then, and only then, should you bring in Hemingway. This ensures your natural voice isn't stifled during the writing process.

In Conclusion: Remember that scene in the movie where the main character discovers a secret weapon that changes everything? That's Hemingway Editor for your essays. It's the game-changer you didn't know you needed. And Jodi? She's now known as the 'Essay Whisperer' in her cohort. A transformation, all thanks to a few well-spent hours with Hemingway.

Writing, like any art, is refined over time. Tools like Hemingway Editor are just catalysts in that transformative journey. Happy writing!

HACK FOUR

Unveiling StuDocu: The Academic Goldmine Every Student Needs

We've all been there. The night before a big test, scrambling to find that one lecture note or desperately seeking a sample essay for inspiration. Enter the realm of StuDocu, a revelation so magnificent it's changing the academic game.

THE REAL STORY:

The vibrant world of TikTok isn't just for dance-offs and viral challenges. Somewhere amidst those trending videos, @bilan.caliii unearthed an academic treasure trove: StuDocu.com. It wasn't portrayed as just another student aid; she pitched it as the lifeline every student had been searching for.

DIGITAL CHRONICLES:

In between the quick dance routines and viral challenges on TikTok, @bilan.caliii's revelation resonated like a clarion call. "Imagine a place," she exclaimed, "where any university, any module you're enrolled in, has its arsenal of resources. That's StuDocu for you!"

The StuDocu Universe: A Closer Look

Tailored University Resources:

StuDocu isn't about the generic one-size-fits-all approach. Enter your specific university and course, and you're presented with a bespoke collection of resources just for you.

Comprehensive Lecture Notes:

Whether you missed a class due to illness or maybe got caught up in another student activity, StuDocu has your back. With an array of lecture notes spanning various modules, you'll never feel out of the loop.

Essay Toolkit:

Beyond just sample essays, StuDocu offers structural guidelines, topic inspirations, peer-reviewed examples, and even critical feedback from fellow students.

Tutorials that Engage:

The platform goes beyond traditional reading materials. With interactive tutorials and discussion forums, it ensures a 360-degree understanding of topics.

Revision Haven:

From mock tests, model answers, and mnemonic flashcards to comprehensive revision plans, StuDocu is your steadfast companion, especially when exams are right around the corner.

The Power of Peer Contributions:

This isn't a platform run by detached professionals. The core of StuDocu lies in its community. Students, having grappled with the same academic challenges, share their nuggets of wisdom.

EXPERT INSIGHTS: GLEANED FROM @BILAN.CALIII'S TIKTOK SPOTLIGHT

- Engage, Don't Just Browse: StuDocu's resources are vast. Instead of mindlessly scrolling, engage with the content. Highlight, annotate, and make side notes.
- Be an Active Community Member: StuDocu thrives on give-and-take. If you've got an essay that received accolades or notes that helped you top the class, share them. Your contribution could be another student's saving grace.
- Master the Advanced Search: With so much to offer, navigating can be daunting. Use advanced search options, filter by academic level, or even by upload date to zero in on what you need.
- Feedback is Gold: Stumble upon a resource that clarified a complex topic? Leave a review. It not only aids others but also uplifts quality content.

The Bigger Picture: At its heart, StuDocu is more than a platform; it epitomizes collaborative learning. It's a testament to the idea that when students come together, sharing their insights and resources, academic success isn't just an individual journey; it becomes a collective triumph.

Wrapping Up: The next time academic panic sets in or when you're striving for that extra edge, remember the invaluable advice from @bilan.caliii's TikTok. With StuDocu, the world of academia isn't just at your door; it's inviting you in for a grand tour.

HACK FIVE

The Research Rundown: Diving Deep into Academic Reading

The life of a student isn't just lectures, essays, and exams; it's also about navigating the vast ocean of academic resources. With countless articles, journals, and publications available, where does one even begin? Well, as always, we've got the inside scoop!

THE REAL STORY:

Every student knows this scenario: You're tasked with writing an essay or research paper, and the professor casually mentions, "Ensure you have a variety of sources." Suddenly, the vastness of the internet seems both a blessing and a curse. But fear not, for we've streamlined the top platforms to elevate your research game.

PROQUEST: THINK OF PROQUEST AS YOUR DIGITAL MEGA-LIBRARY.

From dissertations, newspapers, journals to valuable reports, it's got it all. Spanning across various disciplines, ProQuest offers content from over 90,000 academic publishers. Here's how to make the most of it:

- Thesis Treasure Trove: Looking for dissertations or theses? ProQuest Dissertation & Theses Global is the world's most comprehensive curated collection.
- Subject Specific Searches: Filter your research by disciplines, ensuring you delve deep into the most relevant materials.
- Stay Updated: With new content added continually, set up alerts for specific keywords or topics to keep abreast of the latest publications.

GOOGLE SCHOLAR: GOOGLE'S ACADEMIC SIBLING, GOOGLE SCHOLAR, OFFERS A VAST ARRAY OF SCHOLARLY ARTICLES, FROM CASE LAW TO SCIENTIFIC PAPERS.

- Citation Simplified: One standout feature is its 'Cite' button. Click on it, and you get instant citations in APA, MLA, Chicago, and Harvard formats.
- Integrated Library Linking: Connect Google Scholar with your university library. This way, you can directly access articles that your institution subscribes to.
- Explore Related Works: Found a pivotal article? Click on the "Related Articles" link beneath the search result to explore more in the same vein.

SCIENCE DIRECT: FOR THOSE INCLINED TOWARDS SCIENCE AND TECHNOLOGY, SCIENCE DIRECT IS YOUR BEST MATE. THIS PLATFORM BOASTS OVER 2,500 PEER-REVIEWED JOURNALS AND MORE THAN 11,000 BOOKS.

- Personalized Recommendations: Based on your reading history, Science Direct curates a list of articles that might pique your interest.
- Download High-Quality PDFs: No more dealing with pixelated or watermarked research papers. Science Direct ensures you get premium quality downloads every time.

MEDHUB: A HAVEN FOR MEDICAL STUDENTS AND PROFESSIONALS. MEDHUB PROVIDES IN-DEPTH ARTICLES, CASE STUDIES, AND LATEST MEDICAL RESEARCH.

- Interactive Modules: Beyond just reading, MedHub offers interactive learning modules, perfect for grasping complex medical concepts.
- Collaborative Learning: Join discussion forums to discuss recent findings, share insights, or even collaborate on research projects.

Why It Works: These platforms aren't just about providing content. They're designed to streamline your academic research, ensuring you get quality, relevant, and up-to-date materials. With tailored recommendations, citation tools, and interactive features, they turn the daunting task of research into a structured and engaging process.

Nailing academic research is a fine art. And in the digital age, it's not about accessing information; it's about accessing the right information. Let's delve deeper into the recommended platforms through the eyes of our student avatars.

Dilemma

Edinburgh's chilly evenings often found Jay engrossed in personal letters of WWII veterans, inherited from his grandfather, a WWII hero. Yet, he struggled to contextualise these intimate accounts within the broader historical narrative.

ENTER PROQUEST:

Jay's discovery of ProQuest added depth to his familial connection with WWII, seamlessly weaving personal stories with global events.

MASTERING PROQUEST:

Keyword Crafting:

- Initially overwhelmed, Jay combined broad terms with specific events or places mentioned in his grandfather's letters, e.g., "D-Day landing diaries" or "Battle of Britain personal accounts".

Thematic Searches:

- Jay explored thematic searches such as "daily life in WWII" to understand the backdrop of his grandfather's experiences.

Filtering Tools:

- ProQuest's advanced filters, like date range and document type, helped Jay narrow down time-specific articles or primary source materials.

Stay Updated:

- Jay joined ProQuest's community forums, connecting with other history enthusiasts and sharing resources, insights, and newly discovered stories.

Dilemma

Dilemma: Steve's final year revolved around a mock trial involving historical land disputes. He needed to trace legal decisions, but his university library's collection was insufficient.

SOLUTION WITH GOOGLE SCHOLAR:

This platform revealed layers of legal precedents, turning Steve's fledgling arguments into robust legal contentions.

STRATEGIES ON GOOGLE SCHOLAR:

Year-wise Filtering:

- Steve began by tracing the earliest references to the land dispute, then moved chronologically to understand legal evolutions.

Jurisdictional Awareness:

- Keeping in mind UK laws, Steve used Google Scholar's region filter, focusing on UK legal decisions and interpretations.

Alerts:

- Steve set up alerts for phrases like "UK land dispute precedents" to receive updates on new case laws, scholarly articles, or discussions.

Connect with Local Libraries:

- Google Scholar's library integration meant Steve could directly access full-text versions from Northumbria's subscribed journals.

Dilemma

Growing up near the Thames, Annabel witnessed its changing tides and the effects of climate change. Now, she needed comprehensive data to support her local observations with global scientific consensus.

SCIENCE DIRECT TO THE RESCUE:

Annabel transformed her childhood observations into academically rigorous conclusions.

TACTICS ON SCIENCE DIRECT:

Focused Journal Searches:

- Annabel shortlisted renowned environmental science journals, periodically reviewing their latest publications.

Interactive Visualisations:

- She immersed herself in interactive graphics, contrasting global data with her Thames observations.

Stay Connected:

- Annabel created a Science Direct group, inviting her LSE peers. This collaborative space facilitated resource sharing, discussions, and collective learning.

Personalised Recommendations:

- By rating and saving articles, Annabel received more tailored content suggestions, streamlining her research process.

Dilemma

Max's world turned upside down when his grandmother's shaky hands were diagnosed as Parkinson's. Beyond the emotional turmoil, he grappled with medical jargon and wished to empower himself with knowledge.

MEDHUB'S HEALING TOUCH:

MedHub demystified Parkinson's for Max, providing clarity amidst the chaos.

MEDHUB EXPLORATION:

Disease-specific Modules:

- Max began with Parkinson's-specific modules, understanding its biological and neurological underpinnings.

Engage in Webinars:

- MedHub's live sessions with experts gave Max real-time insights and allowed him to ask personal queries.

Discussion Forums:

- Max started threads about balancing emotional support with medical knowledge, fostering rich discussions and shared experiences.

Stay Notified:

- Subscribing to Parkinson's related updates, Max ensured he was always in the loop about the latest medical advancements or patient care techniques.

HACK SIX

Unravelling the Paraphrasing Puzzle: QuillBot to the Rescue

Manchester's cobbled streets resonate with more than just history; they're alive with the pulsing beats of its local music scene. In one of its dimly lit pubs, with worn-out velvet chairs and wooden tables sticky from spilled ale, you'd find Lily. With her fingers caressing the strings of her guitar, she'd pour her heart out in soulful melodies, capturing the essence of life's highs and lows. These intimate gigs, in small venues filled with locals seeking a brief respite from their routines, were her refuge.

THE REAL STORY:

Yet, amidst this world of heartfelt chords and poignant lyrics, lay Lily's academic life. Studying marketing at university, she found herself frequently overwhelmed with the tedious task of paraphrasing content. Instead of crafting lyrics, she'd be wrestling with words, trying to make them sound original without losing their core essence.
Enter QuillBot.

It was during one of these frustrating nights that a friend, seeing her struggle, introduced her to this online tool. And what a revelation it was!

Lily's Personal Playbook for QuillBot:

- Intuitive Interface:
  - First Glance: Lily was a tad wary of online tools, given her limited tech-savviness. But with QuillBot, all she needed to do was visit quillbot.com.
  - The Process: She'd paste her paragraph into the textbox. A simple click on 'Paraphrase', and in moments, her text was reimagined, ready for use or further edits.
- Adjusting Modes for Tailored Results:
  - Experimentation: Lily spent some time initially playing around with QuillBot's various modes.
  - Creative Flair: Whenever her essays needed some flair or she wanted to avoid repetitive phrasing, the 'Creative' mode was her go-to.
  - Structured Academics: For assignments demanding strict academic tone and structure, she'd rely on the 'Standard' mode to ensure clarity and coherence.
- Breaking It Down for Precision:
  - Challenging Length: Confronted with lengthy, complex sentences, Lily realized that breaking them into shorter segments before inputting into QuillBot often yielded clearer, more concise paraphrases.
  - Segmented Approach: This technique allowed her to maintain control over the content and ensure each part was paraphrased to her satisfaction.

Lily's Personal Playbook for QuillBot:

- <u>Personal Touch – The Final Polish:</u>
  - QuillBot as a Starting Point: She viewed QuillBot as her initial draft creator. Post-paraphrasing, she would infuse her voice and style, ensuring it aligned with her assignment's requirements.
  - Grammar and Flow: Lily also ensured that the paraphrased content maintained grammatical accuracy and flowed seamlessly with the rest of her writing.
- <u>Synonym Exploration for Nuanced Expression:</u>
  - Diction Dilemmas: Sometimes, certain paraphrased words seemed out of place or too repetitive.
  - Word Alternatives: Hovering over these words, QuillBot would provide synonym suggestions. This feature allowed Lily to select words that better matched the tone and intent of her essays.
  - Contextual Checks: While the synonym tool was handy, Lily always made sure her selected word made sense within the overall context.

QUILLBOT'S IMPACT ON LILY'S LIFE:

This wasn't about making life easy; it was about balancing passion and responsibility. QuillBot helped Lily retain her academic integrity while freeing up precious hours, allowing her to strum her guitar, write her lyrics, and continue serenading those cosy, beer-scented corners of Manchester.

HACK SEVEN

Spaced Repetition – Dancing With the Forgetting Curve

Right, brace yourself for a nugget of wisdom, folks!

Enter the 'Forgetting Curve'. Sounds ominous, doesn't it? Picture this: you've just gulped down a chunk of knowledge. Yet, as days go by, that information starts slipping, like sand through your fingers. This curve is basically a graph plotting how our memory of new stuff weakens over time. But wait, before you throw your hands up in despair, here's where the magic happens: the art of spaced repetition.

Instead of cramming everything the night before an exam (admit it, we've all been there), space out your study sessions. It's all about reviewing the material at gradually increasing intervals. Had a lecture today? Review your notes tomorrow. Then, maybe after three days, revisit them. A week later? Give them another glance. Each review session reinforces the information, and like a trusty anchor, it keeps that knowledge firmly in place.

Now, you might be thinking, "Sounds fab, but how do I keep track of all these intervals?" Aha! Welcome to the 21st century, mate. Apps like Anki and Quizlet are your best pals here. They automate the whole process, reminding you what to review and when. No more guessing games!

In the wise words of a random philosopher we just made up: "To dance with the forgetting curve is to tango with time." And trust us, with spaced repetition, not only will you be leading that dance, but you'll also have the confidence that your hard-earned knowledge won't just vanish when you need it most. So, why not give those all-nighters a miss and ensure the info stays put for the long haul? After all, smart study isn't about how hard you hit, but how smart you hit!

Alright, so now that we've got your attention about the magic of spaced repetition, let's delve into these digital wonders that'll help you harness its power.

01 ANKI
YOUR PERSONAL MEMORY COACH

Setting Up:

- Start by downloading the Anki app to your device.
- Set up an account to sync your cards across all devices – laptop, phone, tablet.

Creating Decks:

- Think of decks as subjects or modules. For example, you might have separate decks for "Biology - Cell Division" and "History - Tudor Monarchy".
- Click on 'Create Deck' and give it a snazzy name.

Making Cards:

- Dive into your deck and hit 'Add'.
- Here's where the fun begins. There are loads of card types, but let's stick with the basics for now. One side of the card is your 'question' and the other is your 'answer'.
- Say, you're studying Spanish. Question: "How do you say apple in Spanish?" Answer: "Manzana".

Study Sessions:

- Anki automates the spaced repetition bit. When you review a card and get it right, Anki will schedule it to reappear after a longer interval. Get it wrong? It'll pop up sooner.

Customisation:

- Anki's strength is its flexibility. You can add images, sound clips, and even customise card layouts. Dive into the Anki community online, and you'll find a plethora of shared decks and card styles to help streamline your studies.

02 QUIZLET
FLASHCARDS & MORE

Hop On Board:

- First, either hit up their website or grab the app.
- Make an account. This way, you can access your cards from anywhere.

Creating Sets:

- In the Quizlet universe, 'sets' are akin to Anki's decks. They're groups of flashcards on a particular topic.
- Hit 'Create', and let's get the ball rolling.

Card Creation:

- Simplicity is key here. One side is your term (think of it as the question), and the other is the definition (your answer).
- Using our Spanish example: Term: "Apple", Definition: "Manzana".

Keep Track with Classes:

You can group multiple sets into a 'Class'. Perfect for keeping all your modules neatly organised.

Study Modes:

- Quizlet spices things up with varied study modes. Flashcards are the classic choice, but there's also 'Learn', 'Write', 'Spell', and 'Test'. Each offers a different way to engage with the material.
- Their 'Gravity' game is particularly fun, turning study into a space-themed game. Talk about learning at the speed of light!

Both these tools have a shared goal: making your learning stick. It's about efficiency and effectiveness. No more cramming or last-minute panic sessions. With Anki and Quizlet at your side, you've got the weaponry to conquer the forgetting curve and come out on top. So, dive in and make them work for you!

02 Chapter 2 - Budgeting and Saving Money

Alright, pals, listen up!

Now, before you start wondering why we're diving into the murky waters of budgeting and finances right off the bat, let me spill the beans. We ain't here to just yammer on about counting pennies and being tighter than last semester's jeans. Nope, we're diving deep 'cause money matters. It's the grease that keeps our student life wheels turning, ain't it?

Look around you. We're a generation that's juggling wants and needs like a pro. Dreaming of that summer festival ticket but also need that pricey textbook? We've been there. Torn between Friday night takeaway and saving for post-grad travels? Oh, we feel ya.

This chapter? It's all about striking that balance. We're living in times where a cheeky meal deal isn't just lunch; it's an art of stretching that quid. Our generation is savvy, resourceful, and damn creative when it comes to getting bang for our buck.

So, before you start daydreaming of swanky dinners while you're scoffing down instant noodles, give this chapter a whirl. We're here to make sure you don't just survive on a student budget, but you thrive. Whether it's your first taste of freedom or you're a seasoned pro looking to level up your finance game, we've got you covered.

Money might not buy happiness, but a bit of budgeting savvy can get you closer to those dreams without the constant panic. Let's roll up those sleeves, dive in, and make that student loan stretch like never before! Onwards, my thrifty comrades!

HACK ONE

Student Discounts: Living the High Life on a Shoestring

Alright, my uni comrades, gather 'round!

You know the drill: you grind through the week, surviving lecture marathons, churning out essays at the speed of light, and by the time the weekend arrives, you dream of a little splurge. Perhaps it's that slick leather jacket from Camden Market or the latest gaming headphones? Yet, as you're about to treat yourself, your bank account throws some shade. Ah, the student saga.

THE REAL DEAL:

UK's bustling high streets? They're nothing short of a seductive trap. Today, it's New Look showcasing its autumn collection, tomorrow it's Boohoo dropping a tempting online sale. And, bam, just as you're set to checkout, the discount vanishes. Feel like you're being had? Yep, join the club.

DEEP DIVE INTO THE DISCOUNT WILDERNESS:

Settle in, pals. Navigating student discounts can sometimes feel like steering through a dense fog. One day, brands are all lovey-dovey, showering deals. The next? Absolute radio silence.

STRATEGISING THE DISCOUNT REALM

ALERTS - YOUR BARGAIN BAT SIGNAL:

The digital age offers myriad wonders, and for bargain hunters, alerts are a godsend. Enter James, a third-year student from Liverpool, who learned the value of a timely ping.

It all started when James missed out on an epic ASOS sale. Those trendy jeans he'd been mooning over for weeks? Slashed to half price, and he was none the wiser. The regret was real. But, every cloud and all that. This minor setback had James vowing to always stay in the loop.

James's Guide to Digital Vigilance:

- Setup & Forget: James made it a ritual. Visit the website, hunt for the 'Notify Me' or 'Alerts' option, set it up, and relax. Whether it was a flash sale, new stock, or a restock, he was always in the know.
- Email Categories: To avoid his main inbox getting swamped, James set up a separate category for sale alerts. A quick glance would show if anything enticing popped up.
- Tailored Alerts: Some platforms even allowed James to set specific criteria. Hunting for sports shoes? He'd get pings only for those, not the entire men's section.

Now, thanks to these digital bat signals, those jeans weren't just in his dreams, but on his person.

MAXIMISING DISCOUNT PLATFORMS:

Lucy from Bristol University became the de facto discount queen in her dorm. How, you ask? Two words: UNiDAYS and Student Beans. These platforms became her secret weapons, gateways to a world of slashed prices.

Lucy's Discount Playbook:

- Diverse Categories: Beyond the realms of fashion, Lucy explored tech deals, nabbed dining discounts, and even found cut-price travel deals. That GoPro for her summer trip? 25% off!
- Regular Checks: With deals constantly updating, Lucy ensured she checked in at least once a week. Her diligence meant she rarely missed out.
- Refer and Earn: Lucy spread the love. Recommending friends gave her bonus points or exclusive deals.

SALES SEASONS – THE GOLDEN WINDOW:

David from St. Andrews had an eye for luxury. But, he wasn't about to fork out full price for that swish watch. Instead, he patiently lurked, awaiting sales seasons.

David's Shopping Spree Strategy:

- Calendar Alerts: David marked his calendar with major sale dates. Black Friday, Cyber Monday, Boxing Day sales — he was ready.
- Early Bird Catches the Worm: Some sales offered early access to members or newsletter subscribers. David ensured he was one.
- Wishlist Ready: Instead of frantic last-minute browsing, David had his wishlist prepped. When the sale hit, he was just a click away from a bargain.

SOCIAL MEDIA - THE UNSUNG HERO:

Gemma from Cardiff University had a revelation. Her social media scrolling wasn't just about memes or celeb gossip. It was a treasure hunt.

Gemma's Social Strategy:

- Engage & Win: By actively commenting on her favourite brand's posts or entering their mini-contests, Gemma became a noticeable follower. And brands? They loved her for it.
- Story Stalking: Many brands teased exclusive codes or flash sales on their Instagram or Snapchat stories. Gemma kept her eyes peeled.
- Influencer Collabs: Gemma followed key influencers related to her favourite brands. Their sponsored posts often had exclusive discount codes.

THE WAITING GAME:

Sophie, mastering her subjects at Exeter, added another feather to her cap — mastering online shopping. Her trick? Play hard to get.

Sophie's Sly Shopping Steps:

- Tempt & Retreat: Sophie would add items to her online basket but wouldn't check out immediately.
- Patience Pays: Often, brands nudged her with discounts to complete her purchase. Was it manipulative? Maybe. Did Sophie love the extra discount? Absolutely.
- Incognito Browsing: Sometimes, revisiting items showed a price bump. Browsing in incognito mode ensured Sophie always saw the real deals.

LOYALTY ISN'T JUST FOR DOGS

LET'S GET INTO THE NITTY-GRITTY. GONE ARE THE DAYS WHEN LOYALTY CARDS WERE RESERVED FOR YOUR PARENTS' GENERATION. TODAY, IT'S A SAVVY STUDENT'S SECRET WEAPON. WHY PAY FULL PRICE WHEN LOYALTY CAN SLICE OFF THOSE PESKY POUNDS?

<u>Waterstones</u>: As our Leicester lad Mike discovered, being a regular doesn't just mean getting the nod from the barista. Every coffee or novel he bought added to his points tally. It wasn't long before he was walking out with a free book in hand, all thanks to his consistent visits.

Coffee Craziness:

- <u>Starbucks:</u> Rachel, a caffeine aficionado from Oxford, swears by her Starbucks card. Every sip adds to her star collection. And with enough stars? Hello, free coffee! Plus, they treat you to a drink on your birthday. It's like having a mini party with every latte.

- <u>Costa Coffee:</u> Then there's Birmingham's Danny. Not one to be left out of the coffee loyalty brigade, he found solace in Costa's point system. Every quid he spent turned into points, and soon enough, those frosty winter mornings became a tad warmer with complimentary drinks.

- <u>Caffè Nero:</u> For Sarah from Edinburgh, Caffè Nero's app became her daily ritual. Buying nine drinks? The tenth's on the house. Plus, with their in-app games, sometimes a cheeky extra stamp or two comes her way.

Fashion Fundas:

- <u>H&M:</u> The swanky world of fashion isn't left behind. Mia, a fashion-forward student from London, swears by H&M's loyalty scheme. Every purchase earns her points, and they often throw in exclusive offers, making her wardrobe refreshes a bit lighter on the wallet.

- <u>New Look</u>: Glasgow's own fashionista, Ellie, is all about New Look's loyalty card. With exclusive birthday treats and vouchers throughout the year, it's less about spending and more about saving in style.

- <u>Topshop & Topman:</u> Paul from Manchester made the most of the Topshop & Topman loyalty scheme before they transitioned. Exclusive discounts and early sale access? He was all over it. The landscape keeps changing, so keeping an eye on your favourite brand's loyalty offerings is key.

Eating on the Economical:

- <u>Nando's:</u> Who doesn't love cheeky Nando's? Jess from Newcastle adores it more than most, all thanks to her Nando's card. Every visit, every spicy bite adds up, leading to free dishes. And let's face it, free Peri-Peri chicken? That's a win!

- <u>Subway</u>: Health buff Tom from Norwich makes his subs count. With the Subway loyalty scheme, every sandwich inches him closer to complimentary treats. It's not just about eating; it's about earning with every bite.

And this is just the tip of the iceberg. Nearly every high-street brand out there has caught onto the loyalty game. From Boots to Superdrug, from WHSmith to Greggs, the opportunities are vast and varied.

Moral of the story? If you're a regular somewhere, make sure you're being rewarded for it. Loyalty schemes are like a secret handshake — a nod from brands saying, "Thanks for sticking around. Here's a treat." And as students, we take every treat we can get, right? So, swipe, stamp, collect, and save.

SHARING IS CARING:

Ever heard the saying, "Good things come to those who share"? Well, in student-ville, that's gospel.

NETFLIX AND BUDDY-CHILL:

Jessica from Sheffield was on the cusp of surrendering to a pricey Netflix subscription when the bulb lit up. Why not share? She approached her flatmate, who was about to splurge on Prime Video. The deal? They'd split the Netflix cost, and he'd share his Prime. A perfect barter system was born. Not only did this halve their expenses, but movie nights in Flat 7B became legendary with double the options.
But it didn't stop at streaming services.

SPOTIFY DUO:

Emily from Southampton introduced her flatmate to Spotify Duo. Premium tunes without the ads, and all for a slice of the usual subscription fee. Their kitchen parties? Never skipped a beat.

GAMING GALORE:

Tom from Birmingham and his gamer gang combined their resources for shared gaming subscriptions like Xbox Game Pass and PlayStation Plus. Multiplayer sessions with the newest titles, without each of them individually breaking the bank.
The crux? Pool resources, spread the cost, and elevate the fun. With so many services offering shared or family plans, you get more bang for your buck when you buddy up.

ASK, AND YOU SHALL RECEIVE:

Tom's journey at Warwick began with a few surprising revelations. One chilly evening, as he was buying vinyl for his new record player at a quaint shop, he causally asked if they did student discounts. And guess what? A cool 10% off, just like that.
It made him wonder, where else could he get a cheeky discount?

INDIE CAFES:

Morning coffee runs before lectures took Tom to several indie cafes around campus. Flashing his student ID, sometimes he'd snag a free biscuit or even a few pence off his latte.

LOCAL EATERIES:

During nights out, Tom's crew would end up at local kebab or pizza joints. Asking for student deals, more often than not, they'd get an extra portion of fries or a deal on their meals.

QUIRKY SHOPS:

From that vintage store down the lane to the comic book shop across the street, Tom made it a point to inquire about student perks. The result? Discounts, freebies, or at the very least, a heads-up on upcoming sales.

CULTURAL OUTINGS:

Art galleries, indie cinemas, local theatres – Tom quickly learned that many cultural spots offer student rates. All it took was a simple question.

Tom's ethos became a hit in his dorm. Don't assume; always ask. Businesses, especially around university areas, are keen to pull in the student crowd. And sometimes, all it takes is that one question to unlock a treasure trove of benefits. The world might just surprise you with its generosity!

MAXIMISING DISCOUNT PLATFORMS:

Ah, the platforms that are pure gold for students. Platforms like UNiDAYS and Student Beans aren't just discount warehouses; they're experiences waiting to be unlocked. Let's delve deeper into the majestic world of UNiDAYS:

LUCY FROM BRISTOL UNIVERSITY, OUR REIGNING DISCOUNT QUEEN, SHARED HER SPECIAL UNIDAYS HACKS:

UNIDAYS DEEP DIVE:

- Sign-up Simplicity: Start by registering with your student email. Once you're verified, the universe of discounts is at your fingertips.
- Tailored Alerts: No need to wade through irrelevant deals. Set your preferences and get notifications for brands and categories you fancy. That way, Lucy ensured she was first in line when her favourite brands dropped deals.
- App Over Web: Lucy preferred the UNiDAYS app over the website. The app had a more intuitive interface and offered exclusive in-app deals from time to time.
- Sharing the Love: When Lucy found a killer deal, she used the in-app share feature to let her mates know. Because what's a discount if you can't flaunt it and make your friends a tad envious?
- Brick-and-Mortar Benefits: UNiDAYS isn't just for online shopping. Lucy often flashed her UNiDAYS ID in physical stores to get instant discounts.
- Frequent Visits: The deals on UNiDAYS are dynamic. Lucy made it a point to check the app a few times a week. Her mantra? Stay updated, stay stylish, and stay within budget.

LUCY'S UNIDAYS PROWESS MEANT SHE NEVER HAD TO COMPROMISE ON STYLE OR HER WALLET'S HEALTH. WHETHER IT WAS A ZARA SALE OR AN APPLE STUDENT DEAL, SHE WAS ALWAYS A STEP AHEAD, READY TO SNAG THE BEST OFFERS. AND NOW, WITH HER SHARED WISDOM, YOU CAN TOO!

SO, WHILE STUDENT DISCOUNTS MIGHT SEEM LIKE A MINEFIELD, WITH A BIT OF NOUS AND THESE PERSONALISED TALES OF TRIUMPH, YOU CAN MASTER THE ART. DIVE INTO THIS WORLD OF DISCOUNTS, STRATEGISE YOUR GAME, AND SEE HOW MUCH YOU CAN SAVE WITHOUT SKIMPING ON THE GOOD STUFF. AFTER ALL, A SAVVY STUDENT IS A HAPPY STUDENT!

→

HACK TWO

Savvy Supermarket Shopping: Dining Like Royalty on a Ramen Budget

Alright, folks! Gather 'round the trolley. We're about to navigate the treacherous waters of supermarket shopping. You might be thinking, "It's just shopping, what's the big deal?" Well, brace yourself, 'cause we're about to revolutionise your weekly grocery run.

THE AGE-OLD GROCERY GRIND:

Picture Sarah, a second-year student from Cambridge. Every week, she'd saunter into her local supermarket, grab a basket, and wing it. But come checkout, her wallet would scream in agony. And often, by week's end, she'd find wilted lettuce and expired yoghurt glaring at her from the fridge. Sound familiar?

MASTER THE ART OF MEAL PLANNING:

Sarah's saviour came in the form of meal planning. She realised that mindless shopping wasn't just costly; it was wasteful.

SARAH'S MEAL PREP MANTRAS:

- Plan & Plot: Every Sunday evening, Sarah would sketch out her meals for the week. This wasn't just about dinners; it included breakfast, lunch, snacks - the whole shebang.
- List It: Based on her plan, she'd draft a shopping list. No more impulse buys of chocolates at the counter or that fancy cheese she never ate.
- Adapt & Adopt: Sarah became adept at tweaking her meal plans based on what was on sale. If chicken was at a discount, she'd adjust to include a couple of chicken-based dishes that week.

PRIME TIMES = PRIME SAVINGS:

Did you know supermarkets have secret discount windows? Oh yes! Sarah discovered this goldmine during one of her late evening visits.

HER TWILIGHT SHOPPING TIPS:

- Evening Elves: Most supermarkets markdown perishable items nearing their sell-by dates in the evening. For Sarah, this meant discounted bakery goods, meat, and even dairy.
- Mid-Week Magic: Mid-week visits often had surprise deals. It seems fewer shoppers led to more incentives. Plus, aisles weren't jam-packed, giving Sarah the peace to shop.

THE DIGITAL SHOPPING ASSISTANT - COMPARISON APPS & CASHBACK OFFERS:

In this digital age, shopping isn't just about physical baskets and trolleys. Sarah started wielding her smartphone as her secret weapon.

SARAH'S GUIDE TO SMART DIGITAL SHOPPING:

- Price Spy: Before big purchases, she'd use comparison apps like Price Spy to ensure she was getting the best deal, especially for branded items.
- Cashback Champions: Platforms like TopCashback and Quidco became Sarah's best mates. Every week, she'd check for offers. From a bit of cashback on eggs to discounts on cleaning supplies, these platforms had her back.
- Loyalty Pays: Loyalty cards and associated apps from her frequent supermarkets weren't just for show. They accumulated points, gave exclusive deals, and even birthday freebies.

SARAH'S TRANSFORMATION: FROM A HAPHAZARD SHOPPER TO A SUPERMARKET SAVANT, SARAH'S JOURNEY WAS NOTHING SHORT OF INSPIRING. HER BANK BALANCE WAS HEALTHIER, HER FOOD FRESHER, AND HER WASTAGE MINIMAL. PLUS, THE SAVINGS? THEY WENT INTO HER 'SUMMER GETAWAY' JAR, BECAUSE EVERYONE DESERVES A TREAT, ESPECIALLY WHEN YOU'VE EARNED IT!

HACK THREE

Supermarket Showdown: Where Quality Meets Wallet-Friendly

POP QUIZ :

What do Aldi and Lidl have in common, apart from ending in "i"? They've consistently been the budget-friendly champions for UK students over the past decade. But hang on, before you roll your eyes and think, "Discount means low quality, right?" — park that thought. Let's journey through the supermarket aisles and debunk some myths.

A DECADE OF DOMINANCE:

Research over the past ten years consistently places Aldi and Lidl as the forerunners in the affordability game. But here's the kicker: it's not just about price. These supermarkets have raked in awards for their wine, cheese, and even their steaks. Yes, you heard right, award-winning grub at student-friendly prices!

A CLOSER LOOK: THE ALDI & LIDL PHENOMENON

- Private Labels Galore: A significant chunk of Aldi's and Lidl's products are their own brands. Not only does this reduce costs, but it also ensures a level of quality control.
- Lean and Mean: Their store layouts are no-fuss and efficient. You might not get 20 types of pasta, but you'll get quality choices that do the job. Fewer choices mean quicker shopping trips — perfect for the student on the go.
- Special Buys: Sarah, from our earlier tale, had an alarm set for Aldi's and Lidl's weekly Special Buys. From kitchen gadgets to winter wear, these offers are golden and often comparable to high-end brands.

BUT WHAT IF I WANT A BIT OF

M&S Luxury?

HERE'S THE THING

being budget-savvy doesn't mean you can't indulge now and then. Supermarkets like Waitrose, M&S, and Sainsbury's have their charm, offering exclusive products that are drool-worthy. The key is balance.

Consider doing the bulk of your shopping at discounters like Aldi and Lidl, but top up with specialty items from other supermarkets. Craving that M&S truffle mayo? Go for it! Just make sure your basic groceries come from the more wallet-friendly stores.

BLEND YOUR BASKET

TRENDS OVER THE YEARS:

While Aldi and Lidl have remained consistent favourites, the last decade has seen other supermarkets vying for the student pound. For instance:

- Tesco's Clubcard Prices: These exclusive deals for Clubcard holders have made Tesco a worthy contender.
- Asda's Rollbacks: Periodic price slashes, especially on branded goods, have garnered them a faithful following.
- Morrison's "More" Card: Offering points that convert to vouchers, Morrisons has tried to give students more bang for their buck.

FINAL TROLLEY THOUGHTS:

Navigating the supermarket scene is akin to planning a strategy. It's about stretching that student loan without compromising too much on quality. And with the UK's diverse supermarket landscape, there's room to mix, match, and maximise your grocery gains.
In the wise words of a savvy shopper: "It's not about where you shop, but how you shop." And with this guide, you're well on your way to becoming a supermarket superstar!

HACK FOUR

Too Good To Go: Rescue Meals, Save Money, Save the Planet

Grab a seat and a snack (preferably a rescued one!) and tune in. Here's a tale of Ben, a student with wanderlust in his veins, and how an app became his culinary saviour both abroad and back home.

BEN'S SUMMER DILEMMA:

Ben, a sun-soaked lad, experiencing the best of American summer camps. From late-night bonfires to kayaking adventures, it was the stuff of dreams. But as the days rolled by, his travel budget dwindled, and dining out became a pricey affair. With a couple of weeks left and numerous places still on his bucket list, he stumbled upon an app - Too Good To Go.

WHAT'S THE BUZZ ABOUT TOO GOOD TO GO?

This app isn't just another food delivery service; it's a revolution! It targets food waste by allowing you to rescue meals that cafes, restaurants, and even supermarkets would otherwise toss away. And the best part? You get these at a fraction of their original price.

HOW BEN BECAME A FOOD RESCUE RANGER IN THE US:

- Browse & Book: Every evening, Ben would scroll through the app, checking out 'Magic Bags' from nearby outlets. These bags are surprise packages of unsold items. It's like a food lottery, and honestly, Ben was winning every time.
- Pick-up Points: Ben would often align his sightseeing route with pick-up points. After visiting a museum in New York, he'd swing by a bakery listed on Too Good To Go and grab his rescued snacks.

Diverse Delights: From artisanal sandwiches in Brooklyn to gourmet pastries in Manhattan, Ben tasted a range of delights without hurting his wallet.

HERE'S HOW HE ROCKED IT IN NEWCASTLE:

- Student Life Synergy: Between lectures and library sessions, Ben would check the app for nearby deals. Many cafes around uni participated, giving him a smorgasbord of affordable lunch options.
- Sharing is Caring: Realising the savings and eco-friendly aspect, Ben introduced his flatmates to the app. Soon, they had a routine: alternate days to order, ensuring a steady supply of diverse, discounted, and delicious meals for their flat.
- Exploring New Spots: The app also became Ben's gateway to discovering hidden gems in Newcastle. Cafes and eateries he'd never heard of were now on his radar, all thanks to their listings on Too Good To Go.

WHY TOO GOOD TO GO WORKS:

Alright, let's delve deeper into this app that's not just about nabbing nosh on the cheap; it's way more than that. Here's why Ben, and countless students like him, swear by Too Good To Go:

ECO-FRIENDLY IMPACT:

- Planet Saver: Every time you pick up a 'Magic Bag', you're not just getting a meal. You're actively preventing perfectly good food from ending up in landfills. In a world grappling with climate change, reducing food waste is a massive step towards a sustainable future.
- Carbon Footprint: Think about it. All the energy, water, and resources that went into producing that food – rescuing it means all of that doesn't go to waste either. By rescuing a meal, you're indirectly reducing your carbon footprint. Who knew your dinner could be a statement of eco-activism?

DIVERSE OPTIONS TO SATISFY EVERY PALATE:

- Culinary Adventure: The surprise element means you could be tasting something new every time. From Italian pastries one day to a Thai curry the next, your taste buds are in for a global tour.
- Dietary Diversity: More and more outlets are indicating if their 'Magic Bags' cater to specific dietary needs. Vegan? Gluten-free? There's something for everyone. And the diversity ensures you don't fall into the rut of the same student meals. Say goodbye to beans on toast every other day!

FLEXIBLE PICK-UP TIMES:

- Student-Friendly: Let's face it, the student life isn't always a 9-to-5 affair. With varied class times, library stints, and the odd late-night (or early morning) shenanigans, flexibility is crucial. The app's collection windows, often during off-peak hours, align beautifully with student schedules.
- Plan Your Day: Heading to the library near a café listed on Too Good To Go? Perfect! Align your study break with the collection window. Not only do you get a delicious treat to fuel your study session, but you're also being efficient with your time.

IN A NUTSHELL, TOO GOOD TO GO ISN'T JUST ANOTHER APP ON YOUR PHONE. IT'S A LIFESTYLE CHOICE, MERGING SAVINGS, SUSTAINABILITY, AND SCRUMPTIOUSNESS. SO, NEXT TIME YOU'RE WONDERING WHY IT'S TAKING THE STUDENT WORLD BY STORM, REMEMBER: IT'S THE TRIPLE THREAT OF BEING EASY-ON-THE-POCKET, ENVIRONMENTALLY CONSCIOUS, AND EVER-SO-TASTY. IF THAT ISN'T A WIN, WHAT IS?

HACK FIVE

Freezer Fundamentals: Maximise Space, Minimise Waste

Let's set the scene, shall we? You've gone a wee bit overboard on the weekly shop, driven by hunger rather than logic. Your counters are bursting with fresh produce, meats, and even some cheeky baked goods. Or perhaps you rustled up a Sunday roast and are now staring at a mountain of leftovers, wondering, "How on earth am I going to eat all this before it goes off?" Enter the unsung hero of every student kitchen: the trusty freezer.

THE REAL FROSTY DEAL:

Emily, a nutrition student from Glasgow, was no stranger to the 'eyes bigger than the stomach' conundrum. She also had a penchant for buying fruits when on offer. But instead of letting them go squishy, or throwing out excess food, she turned to her freezer, a treasure chest just waiting to be optimised.

WHY EMBRACE THE CHILLY CHARM OF THE FREEZER?

Wave Goodbye to Wastage: Don't let those extra servings of spaghetti bolognese go to waste. Instead, portion them out in freezer-safe containers. Got a hankering for it two weeks later? Just defrost and dig in!

Freshness Locked In: Those strawberries starting to look a tad sad? Freeze them! They're brilliant for smoothies. Same goes for other fruits, veggies, and even fresh herbs. Freezing them preserves their nutrients and flavour.

Bulk Buying Buddy: Stumbled upon a killer deal on chicken or fish? Stock up and stash it in the freezer. It'll save you heaps in the long run.

Bread's Best Friend: Sliced bread, bagels, or pastries can all find a second life in the freezer. And the best bit? You can toast slices straight from frozen for a quick breakfast.

EMILY'S CHILLY TIPS & TRICKS:

- Flat Freeze: Soups, stews, or sauces can be poured into zip-lock bags and laid flat to freeze. This saves space and ensures even freezing.
- Label Everything: Using masking tape and a sharpie, always label your food with the date and contents. This helps in easy identification and ensures you consume things while they're still at their best.
- Ice Cube Herb Saver: Got leftover herbs? Chop them up, place them in ice cube trays, cover with water or olive oil, and freeze. Next time you're cooking, pop one out and throw it into your pot or pan.
- Defrost Safely: Always remember to defrost foods in the fridge. It ensures the food remains safe to eat and retains its flavour and texture.

WRAP UP: FREEZING ISN'T JUST ABOUT STORING ICE CREAM OR FROZEN PIZZAS. IT'S A GATEWAY TO PRESERVING THE FRESHNESS AND FLAVOUR OF A PLETHORA OF FOODS, ENSURING YOU'VE ALWAYS GOT INGREDIENTS ON HAND AND HELPING YOUR BUDGET STRETCH FURTHER. SO, NEXT TIME YOU'RE ABOUT TO TOSS OUT THAT OVERRIPE BANANA OR LEFTOVER CURRY, THINK TWICE. YOUR FREEZER, MUCH LIKE A MAGIC PORTAL, CAN GIVE THEM A DELICIOUS SECOND LEASE OF LIFE!

HACK SIX

Transportation Triumphs

Make Every Journey Count. Without Emptying Your Pocket

Grab your bags and put on those comfy shoes, we're embarking on a journey into the world of savvy student transportation!

THE REAL TRACK-RECORD:

Picture Cal, a bubbly second-year history student, York University. Originating from the bustling city of London, he often found himself taking the train home, be it for a wholesome Christmas dinner, cracking Easter eggs, celebrating his mum's 50th, or just boogying down on a mate's 21st. But the cost of these journeys? Phew, it almost derailed his student budget!

DOING THE MATH:

Cal did a quick tally. Four trips from York to London in a year (Christmas, Easter, mum's birthday, and that unmissable 21st) at an average of £80 a return ticket would set him back a staggering £320! Enough to fund several cheeky nights out or even a short international getaway.

CHAMPIONING THE RAILCARD:

And then, like a shining beacon in the gloom, he discovered the magic of student railcards.

LET'S BREAK IT DOWN:

- 16-25 Railcard: For just £30 a year, this card offers a whopping 1/3 off rail fares. Simple math time! That £320 for Cal's trips? It comes crashing down to around £213. That's an easy £107 saved! Enough to treat himself (and perhaps his mates) to a lavish dinner or score some epic gig tickets.
- Statistics Speak Volumes: Surveys suggest a good chunk of students travel back home for major holidays and events. If you're among the 60% (made-up statistic for illustrative purposes) of students who hop on a train multiple times a year, the savings from a railcard are evident.

BEYOND THE RAILS:

While trains are all well and good, Cal also realised the world of student transport savings doesn't end there.

BIKE SCHEMES – PEDAL YOUR WAY TO SAVINGS AND FITNESS:

Let's switch gears for a moment (pun fully intended) and chat about the two-wheeled wonders gracing our campuses and cities: bikes. For students like Ellie from Cambridge, bikes are the lifeline that keeps the hustle and bustle in check.

THE UNIVERSITY CYCLE CULTURE:

Universities across the UK are increasingly encouraging students to ditch motorised transport and hop onto bicycles. Why? Well, aside from being a swift and nifty way to dodge traffic, there are plenty of perks:

DEDICATED CYCLE LANES:

Ellie found that many universities and their surrounding cities have dedicated bike paths. These aren't just safe; they often cut through scenic routes, making the ride to that 9 am lecture a bit more picturesque.

BIKE HIRE AND SHARING SCHEMES:

Universities like Oxford, Edinburgh, and Brighton have adopted bike-sharing schemes where students can rent bikes at low hourly rates or even on a monthly basis. It's the convenience of having a bike without the commitment or cost of ownership.

MAINTENANCE WORKSHOPS:

Some unis offer regular free or low-cost bike maintenance workshops. Ellie learned how to fix a flat and adjust her brakes, saving her a packet on repair costs.

SECURE STORAGE:

Worried about leaving your bike out? Many campuses now boast secure bike storage areas, some even with CCTV coverage, so your ride's always where you left it.

DISCOUNTS ON GEAR:

Ellie got her snazzy helmet and high-visibility jacket at a fraction of the price through uni-linked offers. Safety first, but saving a few quid while you're at it? Absolute win!

THE ECO-FRIENDLY BONUS:

Every pedal stroke isn't just saving you money; it's cutting down your carbon footprint. With the current focus on environmental sustainability, cycling is a tangible step towards a greener future. Universities often host 'Green Weeks' or sustainability fairs where students can learn more about the eco-benefits of cycling and even score deals on second-hand bikes.

BIKING BEYOND BOUNDARIES:

The benefits aren't just limited to the campus. Ellie frequently joins weekend bike tours, exploring the countryside, and visiting neighbouring towns. It's fitness, adventure, and savings, all rolled into one.

So, next time you're thinking of hopping onto a bus or hailing a taxi for that short trip, consider cycling. It's a ride that pays off in health, wealth, and a bit of good old-fashioned fun. And as Ellie often says, "Why drive when you can thrive on a bike?"

BUS OFFERS – THE HUMBLE HERO ON WHEELS:

Don't just think trains and bikes, lads and lasses. The humble bus – often overlooked, always reliable – is an unsung hero for the cash-strapped student. Especially when you consider the perks many bus companies, like Stagecoach, lay out for students.

STAGECOACH'S DIGITAL WONDER – THEIR APP:

Cal, always on the lookout for deals, quickly jumped onto the Stagecoach bus app when he heard about it in a casual chinwag. And boy, did it revolutionise his bus travels!

Student Saver Passes: This wasn't just a regular bus ticket. The app offered student saver passes which, over the course of a term or an academic year, amounted to

notable savings. Less money on travel meant more cash for the fun stuff.

Real-time Updates: No more guessing games. With real-time updates on bus timings and locations, Cal could perfectly time his exits from the lecture halls, ensuring minimal waiting time at the bus stop. It's like having a sixth sense for bus timings.

Route Planning: New to an area or just exploring? The app's route planner made navigating unfamiliar terrain a doddle. With clear indications of stops and changeovers, every journey felt like a walk – or ride – in the park.

E-Tickets: Cal's phone was always in hand, so the ability to store e-tickets directly on the app was a game-changer. No more fumbling for change or misplaced paper tickets; a quick flash of the phone, and he was aboard.

Exclusive Deals and Notifications: By enabling notifications, Cal was always in the loop about any exclusive discounts, route changes, or updates. No surprises, no setbacks.

FINAL WHISTLE-STOP:

Whether you're journeying across the country or just zipping around town, the key is to stay informed and make the most of student offers. As Cal found out, with a bit of research and the right tools in hand, travelling needn't be a drain on your finances. Safe travels and savvy savings, folks!

HACK SEVEN

Grab a Bargain at Student Sale Events: Sustainable, Stylish, Sensible

The Age-old Dilemma:

Your wardrobe's looking a tad... well, last semester, and you're keen on a refresh. But with student loans taking their sweet time and fast fashion weighing on your eco-conscience, what's a fashion-forward student to do?

THE REAL DEAL WITH UNI SALES:

Enter Olivia, a second-year Art & Design student at Nottingham. One day, while sipping her morning brew, she spotted a flyer pinned to the union board: "Vintage Clothes Sale - This Friday!" Intrigued, she decided to pop in. Little did she know, this was about to become her shopping holy grail.

THE SUSTAINABILITY FACTOR:

Sick of the environmental toll fast fashion was taking, Olivia was keen to try something new. Vintage sales, often organised by student unions, offer clothes that aren't just stylish but are a great nod to sustainability. It's about looking fabulous while ensuring the planet doesn't pay the price.

EASY ON THE WALLET:

Olivia was chuffed to find that many items at these sales were a fraction of high-street prices. With dresses from a fiver and accessories for even less, she could snag an outfit for the price of a meal deal.

UNIQUE FINDS:

One of the main perks? The pieces Olivia found were unique. No more showing up to student parties in the same ASOS dress as three other people. It was her style, authentic and individual.

SALES BEYOND CLOTHES:

But it wasn't just about clothes. Student unions and various uni societies often host other sales, from plant sales (hello, new room decor!) to book exchanges. These events became Olivia's go-to for sprucing up her space on a budget.

MASTERING THE UNI SALE SCENE:

STAY IN THE LOOP:

Join your student union's mailing list or follow them on socials. They're the first to announce upcoming sales, giving you the heads up to mark your calendar.

BE EARLY:

The best bits often get snapped up quick. Olivia's tip? Turn up a tad earlier. Those extra ten minutes might just get you that dreamy leather jacket or a nearly-new textbook.

CASH IS KING:

Many of these sales operate on cash-only terms. Having a tenner in your pocket ensures you don't miss out on a gem.

HAGGLE (POLITELY!):

Remember, these are second-hand sales. If you spot a minor flaw or just feel like trying your luck, a polite haggle might knock a quid or two off.

KEEP AN OPEN MIND:

Don't just look for current trends. Explore. Experiment. That oversized blazer might just be the standout piece your wardrobe's missing.

THE BIGGER PICTURE:

It's not just about fashion. By supporting these sales, students indirectly promote sustainability, discourage wastefulness, and contribute to a circular economy. For Olivia, it wasn't just about snagging a bargain; it was about making a statement.

So next time you spot a poster or hear whispers of a uni sale event, give it a whirl. You might just walk away with a fantastic find, all while saving those precious pounds. Happy hunting!

HACK EIGHT

Accommodation Affordability: Finding Your Home Sweet (Budget-Friendly) Home

LET'S GET COMFY, MATES!

You're about to embark on what might be your first adventure away from the comfort of your family home. It's exciting, but let's face it: accommodation is one of the biggest chunks out of your student budget. Navigating the maze of where to hang your hat (and stash your teabags) can be trickier than a Rubik's Cube after a few pints.

THE GREAT DEBATE: WHERE TO STAY?

Let's break down your options, and believe me, they're as varied as the fillings in a sandwich shop.

University Halls:
Pros:
- Instant Community: Being surrounded by other students, you'll find making friends a breeze. Perfect for freshers.
- All-inclusive: Often, bills are bundled in, so you won't have any surprise costs.
- Close to Campus: Say goodbye to the morning commute!

Cons:
- Pricey: They can be on the steeper side.
- Less Independence: With communal rules and sometimes stricter regulations, you might feel a bit like you're still at school.

Private Rentals:
Pros:
- More Choices: From cosy flats to spacious houses, the world's your oyster.
- Independence: No uni rules here, mate! Just you and your landlord's agreement.

Cons:
- Bills: Usually, you'll have to sort these out separately.
- Maintenance: Any leaky taps or dodgy boilers? You'll have to liaise with your landlord or letting agency.

Shared Accommodations:
Pros:
- Cost-Effective: Sharing means splitting the costs.
- Companionship: Great for those who don't fancy living solo.

Cons:
- Compromises: You'll have to consider others' preferences and habits.

Words of Wisdom

"Always discuss chores and responsibilities before moving in together. Knowing who takes out the bins can save a ton of passive-aggressive notes"

Aaron of Birmingham

UTILITIES AND BILLS – DON'T GET MUGGED OFF!

Once you've picked your palace, the next step is ensuring you're not paying an arm and a leg for your utilities.

Shop Around: Websites like uSwitch or Compare The Market can help you get the best deals on your gas, electricity, and broadband.

Water Saving: Consider getting a water meter, especially if your house has fewer people than bedrooms. It might work out cheaper..

Bundle Up: Some companies offer bundle deals for broadband, TV, and even mobile contracts.

FINAL TWO PENCE:

Finding a place to live while studying can be a rollercoaster, but with a bit of savvy know-how, you can find a spot that feels like home without draining your bank account. So, whether you're a halls aficionado or a private rental devotee, get out there and find your perfect student haven!

HACK NINE

Banking and Finance Fundamentals: Navigate Like a Pro, Not a Novice! Gather 'round, mates!

You're at uni. Independence, freedom, and for the first time, your finances are pretty much in your hands. But let's be honest: when it comes to banking and handling moolah, many of us feel like we've been thrown in the deep end, without a life jacket. Well, fret not. This hack's got you covered from opening that first student account to making sure you don't descend into the treacherous abyss of perpetual overdraft.

SELECTING THE STUDENT BANK ACCOUNT - IT'S NOT JUST ABOUT THE FREEBIES:

Remember when Sarah from Durham got lured in by that free railcard but ended up with a bank account that didn't quite gel with her needs? Let's not make that blunder.

Interest-Free Overdrafts: Most student accounts offer this. But compare the limits. Some banks start low and increase annually. Others give you a hefty sum straight off the bat.

Additional Perks: Yes, freebies are great, but choose ones that make sense. If you're a frequent traveller, that railcard or coach discount is golden. If you're a techie, discounts on gadgets might be your jam.

Mobile Banking Apps: In this digital age, a user-friendly mobile app is crucial. Instant transfers, spending breakdowns, and even saving pots can make your financial life a breeze.

OVERDRAFTS - A DOUBLE-EDGED SWORD:

Ah, the allure of overdrafts. But while it's tempting to view them as 'extra cash', tread with caution.

Understanding Terms: Most student overdrafts are interest-free, but this isn't forever. Know when interest kicks in, and by when you need to pay it back.

Avoiding the Trap: An overdraft should be for emergencies, not your Saturday night takeaway. It's debt, and the sooner it's paid off, the better.

Shifting Banks Post Uni: Once you graduate, some banks covert your account to a graduate one, possibly reducing your overdraft. If the terms aren't favourable, shop around.

TECH TO YOUR FINANCIAL RESCUE:

There's a whole world of apps and tools designed to help you manage your cash better. Here's the rundown:

Budgeting Apps: Tools like Yolt or Money Dashboard can link to your bank account, categorising and breaking down your spending. They give you a clear picture, helping you identify where those sneaky expenses are adding up.

Savings Boosters: Apps like Plum or Chip analyse your spending and automatically save small amounts that you won't miss. Think of them as your digital piggy banks.

Discount Finders: Before splashing out, check apps like VoucherCodes or Honey. They scout the web for the best deals, ensuring you never pay full price unnecessarily.

FINAL WORDS OF FINANCIAL WISDOM:

Look, navigating student finances can feel like you're in a maze. But equip yourself with knowledge, use the tech at your fingertips, and be mindful of where your money goes. Remember, a penny saved is a penny earned. Or in student terms, that's a few more quid towards the next pizza night! 🍕🎉

HACK TEN

Part-time Jobs and Side Hustles: The Dance Between Dough and Degrees

Alright, mates, pull up your comfiest chair!

We've all been there. Those coffees and nights out add up, and before you know it, your student loan's dwindling faster than a pint on a Friday night. Suddenly, the allure of part-time work isn't just about padding your CV, but ensuring your wallet isn't on a starvation diet. But here's the million-quid question: How do you balance earning some cash without torpedoing your studies?

Balancing Act: Studies vs Work Remember Danny from Leeds? First term, he dived headfirst into a 30-hour workweek at a local bar. Result? Missed lectures, subpar grades, and a burnout faster than you can say "hangover". Here's the thing: part-time work is a double-edged sword.

Balancing the Books and the Bucks: Work-Life-Study Synergy

1-Know Your Limits:

- The Sweet Spot: While 10-15 hours a week seems like the golden range for many, it's essential to self-reflect. Some can handle more, some less. Think about your course load, and remember, it's okay to adjust. You know you best.
- Stay Vigilant: During crunch times like exam season or when dissertations loom large, even those 10 hours can feel like a mountain. It's essential to recognise when to pull back.

2. Communication is Key:

- Setting Expectations: Right from the get-go, when you're in that interview or first chat, be clear about your student status. Most employers hiring students know the drill, but a little reminder never hurt.
- Tips for The Talk:
- Be Transparent: Explain your academic calendar upfront. Highlight potential busy periods like exam weeks or project deadlines.
- Offer Solutions: If you anticipate needing time off, propose alternatives. Can you swap shifts? Work extra hours before your busy period?
- Regular Check-ins: Establish a routine, perhaps monthly or bi-monthly, to discuss your availability. It shows initiative and keeps both you and your employer on the same page.
- Revisit and Re-evaluate: University is unpredictable. Maybe you thought you'd be free on Thursdays, but now there's a mandatory workshop. Or perhaps that group project is taking way longer than anticipated. Instead of struggling in silence, approach your employer early, explain the change, and work out a solution together. Most bosses, especially those familiar with hiring students, appreciate the heads-up and are willing to be flexible.

Remember, you're not just juggling work and study; you're also learning invaluable life skills. Time management, communication, prioritisation – these will stand you in good stead way beyond your uni years. So, chin up, communicate clearly, and confidently stride forth into this balancing act.

Lucrative & Flexible Jobs: The Student Holy Grail

- **On-Campus Jobs:**
  - The Roles: Beyond the well-known Student Ambassadors or Library Assistants, campuses often have roles in IT support, fitness centres, or even in admin departments.
  - The Perks: Not only do you pocket some cash, but these roles are often tailored for students, meaning they're understanding about exam periods and study demands. Plus, zero commute time! Wake up, walk a few steps, and you're at work.

- **Barista or Bartending:**
  - The Real Story: Remember Danny? He wasn't alone. Bars and coffee shops, especially those close to campus, are teeming with student staff. Why? They're usually evening jobs, keeping your days free for lectures and nights (late nights) for, well, student things.
  - Tips Galore: If you're chatty and give good service, the tips can seriously boost your earnings. Some bartenders and baristas pocket almost as much in tips as their base wage.

- **Retail:**
  - Where to Look: From giants like Primark and H&M to local boutiques, many are keen to get students on board. They get it - you're in touch with the latest trends and are likely to pull in fellow student customers.
  - Employee Discounts: This one's a biggie. That jumper you've been side-eyeing? Nab it at a fraction of the cost. Some places offer up to 50% off for their staff.
  - Flexibility: Especially during the holiday season, retail hours can ramp up, offering students ample shifts to choose from. Plus, if you're good, there's always the chance of climbing the ladder. Supervisor roles often come with a pay bump.

When considering where to work, always weigh up the hourly rate, expected hours, and any additional benefits like tips or discounts. But most importantly, pick something you'll enjoy. Working during your uni years isn't just about the money; it's about the experience, the people you'll meet, and the memories you'll make.

Digital Era, Digital Earnings

Jasmine from Glasgow is the poster child for modern side hustles. She started off tutoring her juniors in the subjects she aced, all online. Later, she dipped her toes into freelance writing and even dabbled in graphic design on platforms like Upwork and Fiverr. Her takeaway? Flexibility, decent pay, and skills that glisten on a CV.

- Tutoring: Websites like Tutorful or MyTutor let you share your academic prowess, often from the comfort of your room.
- Freelancing: Writing, design, coding - platforms like Fiverr or Freelancer are brimming with opportunities for those willing to hustle.
- Surveys & Reviews: Websites like Qmee or Swagbucks pay for your opinions. It won't make you a millionaire, but it's a low-effort way to pad your funds.

Success Stories & Lessons Learned

Take Aisha from Cardiff. She bit off more than she could chew with a demanding retail gig, leading to sleepless nights and missed tutorials. A switch to online freelancing? Her grades flourished, and so did her bank balance.

Then there's Liam from Belfast. A part-time gig at the uni cafe not only padded his wallet but led to a full-time role post-graduation. It was the perfect blend of work, networking, and learning.

Wrapping it Up:

In the great juggle of university life, a part-time job can be both a lifeline and a potential pitfall. The secret sauce? Knowing yourself, understanding your academic demands, and picking a role that complements, not complicates, your student journey. Now, go forth and hustle wisely! ✸◆■

HACK ELEVEN

Part-time Jobs and Side Hustles: The Dance Between Dough and Degrees

Alright, gang, here's the long game. I know, I know - you're just getting the hang of juggling lectures, pub nights, and maybe that part-time gig. But hear me out. It's never too early to think about your post-uni financial health. Imagine a life where you're not only counting pennies but watching them grow! Time to get clued up.

The Wonderful World of Saving & Investing:

- **Start Small, Dream Big:** No one's expecting you to chuck half your student loan into stocks and shares. But tossing a few quid into a savings account? Totally doable. You might be surprised at how even the smallest savings can snowball over time.

- **Discover Investing:** Meet Anna from Nottingham. Her granddad left her a bit of money, and instead of blowing it all on a summer trip, she tried her hand at simple investment apps. Anna's pot grew by 15% in a year! She's still planning that trip, but now, it's looking a lot fancier. The key? Research and low-risk investments tailored for beginners.

Credit Score: Your Invisible Financial Passport:

- **What the Heck is it?:** Picture this. You want a loan, a credit card, or maybe even a mortgage down the line. Lenders peek at your credit score to see if you're a safe bet. A good score? They'll roll out the red carpet. A dodgy one? Door's that way, mate.

- Building Blocks: So, how do you build this magical score? Start with small, manageable credit. Think a mobile phone contract or a credit card with a low limit. The trick? Always pay on time. Even better? Pay in full.
- Mistakes Happen: Tom from Swansea got a bit too swipe-happy with his first credit card. He missed a couple of payments and worried he'd sunk his score. But with some advice, he set up a payment plan, cleared his debt, and watched his score climb back up. It's about taking responsibility and setting things right.

Top Tips for Financial Flourishing:

We all dream of being that chap who just gets money, right? The one who always seems to have their financial ducks in a row, while others are still trying to figure out if ducks even like rows. Here's a wee roadmap to get you started on your own path to pecuniary prowess.

- **Research is King:**
  - Why? Knowledge, mate, is power. And in the finance game, it's the power to grow your quid.
  - How? Dive into online platforms like MoneySavingExpert or The Motley Fool. They're crammed with tips, from beginner's guides to more advanced investing tactics.
  - Success Story: Lucy from Birmingham University made a ritual of spending Sunday mornings with a cuppa, trawling through these sites. Fast forward two years? She's got a growing portfolio and a tidy savings pot.

Use Student-Friendly Financial Apps:
- Why? These aren't your granddad's ledger books. They're smart, intuitive, and tailored for folks like us.
- How? Apps like Monzo or Starling don't just hold your money; they analyse your spending, set budgets, and even automatically squirrel away savings. Then there's Moneybox, which rounds up your transactions and invests the change!
- Pro Tip: Aaron from King's College loved his nights out. But post-night-out regrets weren't just about that last pint. With the Monzo app, he started setting monthly limits for his pub escapades. More nights out, less financial hangovers.

Seek Advice:
- Why? Sometimes, you need a human touch. A real person to break things down, especially when charts and graphs start making your head spin.
- How? Your uni likely has financial advisors. They're there for you, and they've seen it all: from maxed-out overdrafts to students making their first investment.
- Real Talk: Raj from University of Edinburgh was a bit skint and, frankly, overwhelmed. A chat with his uni's financial advisor not only set him straight on budgeting but introduced him to the world of ISAs. Free advice that was truly priceless.

So there you have it, future finance gurus. With a pinch of curiosity, the right tools, and a wee bit of guidance, you're on your way to making sure your bank account is as full as your pint glass on a Friday night. Cheers!

03 Chapter 3: Time Management - Making Every Tick Count

Alright, gather 'round, my time-troubled pals!

Ever had that sinking feeling, like you're juggling flaming torches, while riding a unicycle, on a tightrope? Uni can be a bit like that, eh? Between lectures, deadlines, socials, part-time jobs, and, oh, those fleeting moments of 'me time', it's a bleedin' circus act! I've been there – glancing at the clock at noon thinking I've got eons, only to blink and find it's somehow midnight with a to-do list longer than a winter night.

But here's the kicker: it ain't about squeezing more hours into the day. It's about squeezing more juice out of every tick and tock. Sounds cryptic? Fear not. By the end of this chapter, you'll be turning time into your best mate, rather than that pesky foe that's always running away from you.

So, if you're keen to dodge the mad, end-of-term scramble and keep things cool as a cucumber, stick around. We've got the lowdown on how to juggle the jigs and reels of student life, without dropping the ball (or the flaming torches). Onwards!

HACK ONE

The Digital Wizardry of Apps

Hold tight, team!

Do me a favour and pull out that shiny pocket-computer of yours. You know, the one that's seen more of your face recently than your mum has? Jessica, a chirpy student from Liverpool Uni, was once just like you, drowning in the pixelated realm of her mobile. But here's where the tale takes a twist.

One frosty evening, as Jess cozied up with a cuppa, she did a wee audit of her phone habits. And oh boy, the numbers were staggering. She was clocking in a whopping 8 hours a day. That's a full work shift, mate! The realisation was a kick up the backside. She decided her device was going to boost her productivity, not bury it.

FOREST

The Lush Path to Laser Focus: Jess got introduced to this beaut of an app from a mate who knew her all-too-well. The idea is deceptively simple. Set a timer, plant a virtual sapling and get cracking with your work. As long as you resist the siren call of other apps, your tree grows. But if temptation wins? Your budding tree wilts and dies, a tragic victim of procrastination.

The quirky concept became Jessica's steadfast study partner. Those little trees were a visual representation of her hard graft. And over time, a dense, verdant forest flourished, mirroring her academic achievements. It wasn't just an app; it was a motivation tool, turning every study session into a green-fingered challenge.

TRELLO

Your Digital Taskmaster: Enter Trello. Jess had group projects, personal assignments, and the rigmarole of uni life to juggle. Post-it notes? Too 2000-late. Spreadsheets? Overcomplicated. Trello's drag-and-drop interface was her saviour. She could categorise tasks, set deadlines, and collaborate seamlessly.

Every card she moved to the 'Completed' column was a mini celebration. It visualised progress, kept her on track, and heck, it even made group projects bearable. It was like having a personal organiser, breaking her mountainous workload into manageable molehills.

GOOGLE CALENDAR

Life's Personal Assistant: Now, this was a revelation. Initially, our Jess used it for the occasional bash or outing. But soon, she transformed it into her personal oracle. Everything went in there - from study group meetings, lecture timetables, to her weekly 'Treat Yo' Self' downtime.

Colour coding became second nature. Blue for academic, green for personal, red for urgent. She synced reminders, blocked out focused study sessions, and had a bird's eye view of her week at a glance. With Google Calendar by her side, she danced through her days with an orchestrated rhythm, missing nary a beat.

THE TURNAROUND

In just a few months, Jessica's daily routines saw a 180-degree flip. The same device that was her biggest distraction became the linchpin of her productivity. Her grades? Skyrocketing. Her social life? Still buzzing. Stress levels? Way down. And that screen time? Halved, but every minute was purposeful.

A lesson from our Liverpool lass? Time management in the digital age isn't about shunning technology. It's about harnessing it, tailoring it, and letting it elevate you. So, next time you unlock that phone, ask yourself: is it going to be a tool or a toy? The choice, mate, is all yours.

HACK TWO

The Pomodoro Technique - Mastering Your Mental Mojo

Ellie, a sprightly History student from York, was on the brink. The sheer volume of readings, essays, and exam prep was enough to send her into a tizzy. It felt like she was sprinting a marathon, and mate, she was knackered. Then, in one of those late-night deep-dives, Scrolling through instagram Reels, she stumbled upon the 'Pomodoro Technique'.

"Pomodoro? Like the tomato?" she thought, bemused.

Indeed, named after the Italian word for tomato, this technique was inspired by a simple kitchen timer. It promised better focus, reduced fatigue, and, well, a life where you're not always gasping for breath.

The Juicy Basics: The concept? Surprisingly straightforward. Work with laser focus for 25 minutes straight, then hit the brakes and take a 5-minute break. Rinse and repeat. Every fourth break is a longer, luxurious 15 minutes. Ellie was sceptical, but desperate times call for desperate measures. She gave it a go.

The Psychological Genius Behind It: What's fascinating about this timer trick is its underlying psychology. See, our brains, fantastic as they are, have their limits. Think of them as muscles; even the best athletes can't sprint endlessly. The Pomodoro Technique taps into this very concept. By working in bursts, you're maintaining an optimum pace – fast enough to get things done, but not so relentless that you burn out.

These time chunks keep the dread of procrastination at bay. Instead of dreading a mammoth 3-hour study session, Ellie only had to commit to 25 minutes. It was mentally manageable, like nibbling on an elephant bite by bite rather than trying to swallow it whole.

Ellie's Evolution: The first week was a game of adjustment. But by day seven? A revelation. Ellie noticed she was breezing through chapters in record time. Those 5-minute breaks became sacred – a quick stretch, a gaze outside, even a cheeky biscuit or two. And the longer breaks? Perfect for a brisk walk or a natter with her flatmate.

Instead of feeling drained at the end of a study day, Ellie felt invigorated, ready to take on a pub quiz or a movie night. Her productivity soared, and her grades? They followed suit.

The Wider Impacts: But the Pomodoro Technique did more than just boost Ellie's study efficiency. It taught her the art of discipline and the value of breaks. She started applying it beyond academics. Chores, hobbies, even her guitar lessons – everything got the Pomodoro treatment.

And here's the kicker: Ellie began to truly value her time. Each Pomodoro became a precious window, an opportunity. It wasn't just about cramming facts anymore; it was about making every second count, both academically and personally.

The Heart of the Matter: At its core, the Pomodoro Technique isn't just a time management hack; it's a philosophy. It acknowledges our human limitations and turns them into strengths. It's about respecting our mental bandwidth, knowing when to push and when to pause.

For Ellie, and countless students like her, the Pomodoro Technique was a lifeline in the choppy seas of university life. It's a testament to the fact that sometimes, the simplest solutions can bring about the most profound changes. So, if you ever find yourself overwhelmed, remember the humble tomato. It might just hold the secret to your success.

HACK THREE

Priority Lists - Mastering Your Time with Modern Tools

Gather 'round, champs, and let's dig deep into that ever-mounting pile of tasks. Ever had that sinking feeling of drowning in to-dos? We're about to throw you a lifeline.

Enter Sarah, an enthusiastic Literature student from Birmingham Uni. Her tasks, like confetti after a grand celebration, were scattered everywhere. Then, amidst a whirlwind of deadlines, she had a brainwave: Why not merge old-school methods with a sprinkle of tech magic?

To the App Store and Beyond!

Sarah wasn't content with scribbling on random bits of paper. She needed structure. This quest led her to the app "Todoist".

TODOIST

A Taskmaster's Dream:

- <u>Getting Started:</u> She downloaded Todoist from the App Store and set up a free account.
- <u>Creating Projects:</u> Sarah categorised her tasks: 'Uni', 'Personal', 'Urgent', and the cheeky 'Maybe Later' for those low-priority items.
- <u>Colour-Coding & Priorities:</u> The app allowed her to assign colours and priority levels, making her list visually intuitive.
- <u>Recurring Tasks:</u> Weekly grocery shopping? Set it as a recurring task. Those repeated chores became automated reminders.
- <u>Karma Points:</u> Todoist gamified task management. Sarah earned points for completing tasks, which kept her motivated.
- <u>Integration:</u> Synced with her Google Calendar, Sarah never missed a beat.

THE MIGHTY WHITEBOARD

But Sarah missed the tactile feel of a physical board. So, she got herself a whiteboard. This wasn't a step back; it was a bridge between the digital and the tangible.

Crafting the Whiteboard Wonderland:
- Zone Creation: She split her board into sections mirroring her Todoist: 'Uni', 'Personal', etc.
- Colour Coordination: Using coloured markers that matched her app's colour scheme, she had visual harmony across both platforms.
- Quick Glance, Quick Update: Every morning, she'd glance at her board, quickly updating or ticking off tasks. The satisfaction of wiping off a completed task? Immense.
- Sticky Notes for Flexibility: Some tasks needed shuffling around, and sticky notes gave her that flexibility.

Bridging the Gap:
Every evening, Sarah updated Todoist based on her whiteboard changes. It became a ritual, almost therapeutic. Her phone gave her reminders on the go, and her whiteboard gave her a broader picture at home.

The transformation? Sarah felt in charge, not just of her tasks, but of her time. She had a roadmap, both digital and physical. It was like having a GPS for her daily grind.
So, mates, if you're feeling swamped, consider this dual approach. Harness the power of tech, but don't forget the charm of the tangible. It's a blend of the modern and the classic, a bit like enjoying a vintage vinyl record on the latest sound system. Perfect harmony.

HACK FOUR

Study Groups & Buddy Systems – Making Academia Social (and Fun!)

Alright, you lot! Get ready to toss that age-old image of a studious loner, surrounded by stacks of books, barely seeing the light of day. We're in the era of collective brainpower. Ever heard the saying, "If you want to go fast, go alone. If you want to go far, go together"? Let's dive into that.

OLIVER'S ODYSSEY:

Oliver, a chirpy History student from the University of York, always thought studying was a solo sport. Until, one gloomy Monday, his mate Aidan introduced him to the world of study groups. The journey from solitude to collaboration wasn't just enlightening; it was downright game-changing.

SETTING UP YOUR STUDY DREAM TEAM:

- The Right Mix: Ollie quickly learned it wasn't just about pulling together his pub quiz team. It was about balance. They needed a mix – someone ace at research, another with a knack for presentation, a tech wizard, and of course, someone with those coveted note-taking skills.
- Clear Objectives: Before diving in, they set clear goals. Was it about tackling a particular assignment? Revising a specific module? Knowing their North Star kept them on track.
- Regular Schedule: A dedicated slot, say every Wednesday evening, ensured consistency. It became a ritual, like Match of the Day, but for academia.
- Swap & Share: They rotated homes or opted for quiet corners in the library. Different environments often spurred different perspectives.

Golden Rules to Keep the Harmony:
- <u>Equal Contribution:</u> Everyone should pitch in. No free riders!
- <u>Avoid Distractions:</u> Phones face down. Periodic breaks, yes. But during grind time? Absolute focus.
- <u>Respect Opinions:</u> There's bound to be disagreements. But remember, it's about understanding diverse perspectives, not winning a debate.
- <u>Celebrate Together:</u> Finished a tough assignment? Time for a cheeky pint or a movie night!

WRAPPING IT UP:

As Oliver discovered, studying needn't be a lonesome endeavour. Collaborative learning can be stimulating, enriching, and yes, a whole lot of fun. From late-night pizza debates on Roman history to animated PowerPoint sessions on modern politics, Oliver's grades didn't just soar; his university experience was transformed.

So, the next time you're dreading a massive assignment or a tough module, round up your crew, or just your best mate. Tackle it together, laugh over the blunders, and celebrate the victories. After all, isn't that what uni life's all about?

HACK FIVE

Time-Blocking and Themed Days – Mastering The Clock & Your Sanity

Alright, mates! Buckle up because we're about to tackle the time monster. Ever felt like days just zoom past with half your to-dos still glaring at you? We've all been there. Enter: Time-blocking and themed days. It's a bit like meal prepping, but for time. Sounds intriguing, right? Let's get stuck in.

ELEANOR'S EPIPHANY:

Meet Eleanor, a sprightly Sociology major from the University of Southampton. On top of her studies, she was juggling part-time work, society commitments, and, well, life. Her days resembled those chaotic comedy sketches - hopping from one task to another, always racing against the clock. But, during a random workshop on 'effective studying,' she stumbled upon the idea of time-blocking and themed days. Initially sceptical, Eleanor decided to give it a whirl. The results? Absolutely transformative.

TIME-BLOCKING 101:

- Understanding Tasks: Eleanor started by jotting down her weekly tasks - assignments, readings, job shifts, society meetings, etc.
- Estimation: She then estimated how long each task might take. Initially, she got it wrong a few times, but soon she was hitting the nail on the head.
- Dedicated Blocks: Using a digital calendar (good old Google Calendar worked wonders), she began assigning blocks for specific tasks. Morning deep study sessions, post-lunch admin tasks, evening for relaxation or social commitments.
- Buffer Zones: Eleanor left small breaks between blocks, ensuring unexpected hiccups wouldn't throw her entire day off course
- Reassess & Adapt: Every Sunday, she'd review her week. What worked? What didn't? Adjustments were made accordingly.

THEMED DAYS – THE GAME CHANGER:

Going a step further, Eleanor dabbled with the idea of themed days.

- <u>Meticulous Mondays:</u> Dedicated to organising - updating her calendar, setting her goals, ensuring her ducks were in a row.
- <u>Deep Dive Tuesdays:</u> No interruptions, just in-depth study sessions, diving deep into subjects.
- <u>Work Wednesdays:</u> Shifts at her part-time job took precedence.
- <u>Society Thursdays:</u> Meetings, events, or planning sessions for the clubs she was part of.
- <u>Freebie Fridays:</u> A flexible day. Could be for catch-ups, leisure, or extra study.

This approach meant her brain wasn't constantly switching gears. It could focus on a theme, making her much more efficient.

TOOLS TO AID THE TIME-BLOCK MAGIC:

- <u>Digital Calendars:</u> Eleanor used Google Calendar for its simplicity and syncing capabilities. Colour-coded blocks gave her a clear visual of her day.
- <u>Apps Like 'Clockwise':</u> They optimise your calendar, moving things around to ensure you get maximum focused time.
- <u>Physical Planners:</u> For those who love writing, planners with hourly breakdowns can be bliss.

Eleanor's uni life saw a 180-degree turnaround. Time-blocking and themed days eliminated the chaos. She had clarity and control. Her grades? Up. Stress levels? Down. Plus, she could make time for a cheeky evening out or a Netflix binge without the guilt.

So, for everyone feeling the crunch of the ticking clock, remember Eleanor's journey. With a bit of planning and discipline, you too can dance to the rhythm of time, rather than racing against it. It's not about cramming more into your day; it's about making every moment count. And with this hack, consider that mission accomplished!

HACK SIX

Mindfulness and Mental Well-being – Nurturing Your Inner Sanctuary

Lend me your ears, troops. We're stepping into territory that often goes ignored in the hustle-bustle of university life: mental well-being. Ever felt like you're constantly racing, heart pounding, deadlines chasing, with the dread that you'll never catch up? If that hits a nerve, this hack's for you. Dive deep with me into the tranquil waters of mindfulness and mental health, and discover how it's about more than just ticking off tasks.

THE BREAKING POINT: OWEN FROM UNIVERSITY OF BRISTOL

Picture Owen, a bright spark pursuing Engineering at the University of Bristol. On the surface, he had it all together—top grades, involved in societies, you name it. But beneath the veneer, Owen was close to breaking. Every little assignment felt like a mountain, the weight of expectations pushing him towards an edge he didn't want to approach.

THE SILENT STRUGGLE OF STUDENTS:

The truth? Many tread water in the same turbulent sea. University, with its challenges, can be both exhilarating and, let's face it, downright scary. The journey of being away from home, meeting deadlines, and navigating social dynamics can be overwhelming. Owen's struggle is a mirror to what many feel but seldom discuss.

THE ENLIGHTENMENT - DISCOVERING MINDFULNESS:

A serendipitous conversation with a counsellor introduced Owen to the world of mindfulness—a practice that trains you to anchor yourself in the present.

WHY MINDFULNESS MATTERS:

- Combatting Overwhelm: Instead of getting drowned in the 'what-ifs' of tomorrow or the regrets of yesterday, mindfulness keeps you grounded in the now.
- Emotional Resilience: It's not about dodging stress but learning to ride its waves without getting pulled under.
- Enhanced Focus: Ever read a page and realised you've absorbed nothing? Mindfulness trains your brain to concentrate on one task at a time.

OWEN'S INITIATIVES:

1. Meditation: It began with just 10 minutes daily, using apps to guide him. Those moments of stillness became Owen's sanctuary from chaos.

2. Mindful Walks: Bristol, with its blend of urban and green spaces, was perfect. Owen would stroll, focusing on the rustle of leaves, the patter of rain, the hum of city life.

3. Gratitude Journal: Every night, Owen noted three things he was thankful for. Over time, this practice shifted his focus from incessant worries to the blessings scattered in his day.

4. Digital Detox: Owen allocated hours where he'd be offline, freeing himself from the constant barrage of notifications, news, and stresses that come with them.

EMPHASISING THE IMPORTANCE OF MENTAL HEALTH:

Owen's story isn't just an individual tale. It's a lesson and a reminder. As students, grades are important, but what's even more crucial is mental health. Without it, even the best grades can feel hollow.

Universities and colleges increasingly recognise this, offering counselling services, mental well-being workshops, and resources. But the first step? Acknowledging that it's okay to seek help. It's okay to admit you're struggling. In fact, it's more than okay—it's brave.

TOP APPS FOR MINDFULNESS & MENTAL WELL-BEING:

- <u>Headspace:</u> From guided meditations to sleep stories, it's a haven for beginners and veterans alike.
- <u>Smiling Mind:</u> Tailored programmes for different age groups, including university students.
- <u>MyLife Meditation:</u> Check in with your feelings, and the app suggests guided meditations based on your mood.

OWEN TODAY:

Owen still faces challenges—after all, life's no fairy tale. But he's equipped to handle them better. No longer a leaf tossed in a storm, he's become the tree—deep-rooted, standing tall through life's trials.

And so, dear reader, remember this: In the frenzy of uni life, take a pause. Breathe. Care for your mind. Because a healthy mind isn't just about facing university—it's about embracing life in all its beautiful, chaotic splendour.

OWEN'S DIVE INTO HEADSPACE: UNPACKING THE EXPERIENCE

When Owen first tapped into the Headspace app, the bright colours and friendly interface greeted him. At first glance, it looked like any other app, but Owen soon realised this could be the tool he'd been missing.

1. Starting with the Basics: Headspace, true to its mission, eases you in. Owen began with the "Basics" pack, a ten-day guided introduction to the world of meditation. Narrated by Andy Puddicombe (co-founder and a former monk!), Owen found himself led gently into understanding the essence of meditation. No jargons, no complexities—just a straightforward guide.

2. Sleep Solutions: One of Owen's challenges was sleep—or the lack thereof. Headspace's 'Sleepcasts' became his nightly ritual. These are 45-minute audio experiences that mix ambient sounds with calming narratives. From a desert journey under starlit skies to a meandering path through a rainforest, these stories transported Owen into tranquillity, leading to more restful nights.

3. Managing Stress: The 'Stress' meditation pack drew Owen's attention next. It's designed to reshape one's relationship with stress, to observe it without getting ensnared. Over the course of 30 days, Owen felt a subtle shift. Those heart-racing moments of panic became rarer. In their place? A calmer perspective that allowed him to navigate challenging situations without being overwhelmed.

4. On-the-Go Mini Meditations: University life can be frantic. For those moments when Owen felt the stirrings of anxiety but didn't have much time, he tapped into Headspace's mini meditations. Ranging from 1 to 3 minutes, these are perfect for a quick reset. Whether before an exam, an interview, or just a chaotic day, these mini sessions became his quick escape hatch.

5. Personalised Experience: What Owen loved was how Headspace tailored suggestions based on his activities. If he'd been doing a lot of stress-related sessions, the app might suggest a calming 'Wind Down' session before bed.

6. Progress Tracking: A motivating feature was the ability to track his progress. Owen could see his 'total time meditated', 'consecutive days' of meditation, and even the 'total number of sessions'. This gave a tangible sense of accomplishment, fuelling his commitment.

Meditation, for Owen, was no longer a distant, mystical concept. With Headspace, it became accessible, doable. The app didn't just introduce him to meditation; it integrated mindfulness into his daily life. Moments of calm, focus, and clarity were no longer rare gems—they became a part of his daily existence.

Diving into Calm, the tranquil backdrop of a serene lakeside surrounded by mountains immediately sets the tone. The app, true to its name, offers a plethora of resources to cultivate inner peace. At its core, there's a daily meditation practice aptly titled 'The Daily Calm'. Each session, around 10 minutes, touches on a unique theme, from managing stress to gratitude. For those seeking better sleep, Calm provides 'Sleep Stories'. Think of them as bedtime tales for adults, narrated by soothing voices, including some celebrity surprises. These stories are intricately designed, allowing the listener to drift into restful slumber, making nighttime anxieties a thing of the past. Additionally, Calm provides masterclasses from experts on topics ranging from breaking bad habits to conscious parenting. It's not just an app; it's a holistic experience.

Insight Timer: A Community of Mindfulness

Venturing into Insight Timer, it's evident that this app is a treasure trove for meditation enthusiasts. With over 70,000 free meditations, there's something for everyone. Whether you're a beginner needing guided sessions or a seasoned practitioner seeking timed meditation with ambient sounds, Insight Timer delivers. What sets it apart is its community-centric approach. Users can see, in real-time, others meditating around the world, fostering a sense of global connectedness. The app also hosts courses spanning various lengths, diving deep into subjects like managing anxiety, cultivating happiness, and exploring mindful eating. An added bonus? The extensive music tracks available, perfect for relaxation, concentration, or even yoga. Insight Timer isn't just a solo experience; it's joining a global family on a collective journey towards well-being.

HACK SEVEN

The Digital Detox – Reclaiming Real Life

Alright, you lot, let's chat. We've all heard it, right? "Staring at screens all day isn't good for you." And while many of us nod in agreement, putting it into practice is a whole different kettle of fish. Enter Cara from the University of Winchester.

Cara, a bubbly sociology major, was the epitome of the modern student. Notes on OneDrive, group chats on WhatsApp, lectures on Zoom, and downtime? Well, that was Netflix's domain. But as the weeks rolled by, Cara found herself increasingly irritable, drained, and – dare we say – a bit disconnected. It wasn't long before she figured out the culprit: her whopping 8-hour daily screen time.

Now, here's the tricky part. For Cara, going off the grid wasn't an option. Uni demanded digital. But she was determined to carve out screen-free chunks in her day. So, began Cara's digital detox journey.

Real-Life Alarms: Cara started setting alarms – not to wake up, but to unplug. Every couple of hours, her phone would chime, signalling a 10-minute screen-free break. Initially, she'd just stretch or gaze out the window, but soon, these breaks turned into mini guitar sessions, quick sketches, or even a jaunt around the block.

The Evening Wind-Down: As sunset approached, Cara made a pact: No screens an hour before bed. Instead, she'd dive into a book, scribble in her journal, or indulge in some old-school board games with her mates.

Digital Sabbatical: Every Sunday, Cara declared a screen sabbatical. Phones, laptops, the telly – everything went off. The first time? It was daunting. But as weeks turned into months, Sundays transformed into adventures – hikes, picnics, museum visits, or even just lounging with a physical newspaper.

Apps to Unplug: Oh, the irony! Cara used apps to reduce her app usage. 'Freedom' was her pick, blocking distracting apps during study hours. Meanwhile, 'Offtime' provided insights into her digital habits, helping her identify and curb time-drainers.

Reinventing Downtime: Instead of mindlessly scrolling through Instagram or diving into a Netflix rabbit hole, Cara started exploring hobbies. Photography, knitting, even pottery – her room is now adorned with quirky clay mugs and vibrant photos of campus life.

By semester's end, not only had Cara's screen time reduced by a staggering 40%, but she felt revitalised. She was more present during conversations, her sleep improved, and, as a surprising bonus, her grades ticked upwards.

Now, here's the kicker. We're not saying chuck your gadgets out the window. Nope. It's about striking a balance, setting boundaries, and remembering there's a big, beautiful, tangible world out there, waiting to be explored. Cara's story isn't unique; it's a call to action. The next move? Well, that's up to you.

04 Chapter 4: Study and Revision Hacks – Going Old-School

Alright, gather 'round, you tech-savvy scholars! You might've noticed that, so far, we've been heavy on the digital – apps, screens, pixels, the lot. But here's a curveball: What if we told you there's magic in the tried-and-true, old-school methods? Now, don't fall off your chairs! We're not suggesting you bin your gadgets and return to the stone age, but sometimes, a sprinkle of the past can jazz up the present in unexpected ways.

You see, not every solution to today's academic puzzles can be found with a swipe or a click. Some secrets lie in the dusty corners of tradition, waiting to be unearthed and given a fresh spin. So, if you've ever romanticised about being a student in the pre-digital era or just want a break from screen glare, this chapter's for you. Fancy acing that exam with just paper, pens, and a dash of ingenuity? Let's get stuck in!

HACK ONE
Flashcards – The Magic of Active Recall and Spaced Repetition

The Real Deal: Meet Max, or "Biggesy" as his mates at Southampton fondly call him. An economics student, Max was your typical crammer – one who thought long hours staring at notes was "studying". Until flashcards entered the scene.

Max began converting his notes into questions and answers, scribbled on palm-sized cards. Before exams, he'd shuffle this deck, testing himself. Each correct answer? Moved to a different pile to be reviewed later. Wrong ones? Reviewed more frequently. Sounds basic, right? But the results were astonishing.

The Science Bit: What Max was unknowingly tapping into were two proven learning techniques – Active Recall and Spaced Repetition. Active Recall is about retrieving information without looking. Every time Max tested himself with a flashcard, he strengthened his memory retrieval paths. It's like going to the gym, but for your brain.

Spaced Repetition, on the other hand, is about reviewing information at increasing intervals. Our brains are more likely to retain information reviewed over spaced intervals rather than crammed in one go – a concept Max's increasing piles of flashcards nailed perfectly.

MAKING IT WORK FOR YOU:

Convert Your Notes: Distil your lecture notes, turning them into bite-sized questions and answers.

Test Yourself: Shuffle the deck and go through each card. Separate them based on what you get right and wrong.

Space It Out: Review the 'wrong' pile more frequently than the 'right' one. As you get better, increase the time between reviews.

Max's transformation wasn't just about a change in method but understanding the psychology behind it. By the end of the semester, not only was he acing his exams, but he also had more free time. Flashcards weren't just a study tool; they were his secret weapon against the cramming chaos. And the best bit? They can be yours too. All it takes is a little understanding and a lot of cards!

HACK TWO

Mind Maps – The Art and Science of Connecting the Dots

The Real Deal: Picture Jake, an English Language student at Durham, surrounded by heaps of notes, essays, and annotations. A veritable mountain of words, phrases, and concepts. One day, overwhelmed, Jake sketched out a central idea on a blank page and began drawing connections from it. He used a rainbow of colours, doodles, even the odd star sticker from his little sister's craft set. What he was doing, though unconsciously, was unlocking a powerful tool of cognition and retention: Mind Maps.

The Science Bit: Our brains don't think linearly; they think in connections. When Jake started creating mind maps, he was doing more than just organising his notes; he was mirroring his brain's natural way of processing information. Every branch, colour, and doodle worked as visual triggers, improving recall. The different colours stimulated different parts of his brain, making the information more memorable. By connecting related concepts, Jake could see the bigger picture, making abstract ideas tangible and easier to grasp.

Mind mapping taps into both the logical and creative hemispheres of the brain. For Jake, an English student, it was the perfect marriage between structured linguistic knowledge and the creative flair of language.

Making It Work For You:
- <u>Start Central:</u> Jot down the main idea or topic in the centre of a blank page.
- <u>Branch Out:</u> Draw lines out from the centre, each representing a main sub-topic or thought related to the central idea.
- <u>Get Colourful:</u> Assign different colours to different branches. It not only makes your mind map vibrant but also makes it easier to navigate.

- Doodle Away: Include little drawings, symbols, or stickers. They act as visual aids, boosting memory recall.
- Link Concepts: Found a connection between two seemingly separate ideas? Draw a line, make a note. These links can be critical in understanding complex topics.

Jake's days of wading through note avalanches were over. Mind maps made him efficient. They helped him link ideas, see patterns, and most importantly, deeply understand his course material. By semester's end, Jake wasn't just acing his papers; he had become the go-to guy for study techniques. And the heart of his strategy? Those radiant, sprawling mind maps that covered the walls of his dorm. As for you, dear reader, give mind mapping a whirl. You might just find, like Jake did, that sometimes, the answer to complexity is a simple drawing.

HACK THREE — Study Spots – Rotation for Inspiration

The Personal Touch: Back in my uni days in Newcastle, I had this cosy nook in Caffe Nero, right by the window. A steaming cup of cappuccino, ambient background chatter, and the soft hum of a city waking up. It was my fortress of solitude. I loved it, truly. Then, there was this local independent café down the lane, oozing that rustic charm and playing soft jazz. But, you know what? Even my favourite spots started to lose their sheen after a while. It became routine. I'd sit down, order my usual, and stare blankly at the same view.

Desperate for a change, I set myself a challenge: four different cafes, one week. Each visit, an hour or two, not more. And, by Jove, it was transformative. Every new café brought with it a new vibe. One day, I found myself amidst a lively debate between baristas about the best chocolate cake recipe. The next, I was surrounded by fellow students, all engrossed in their work, their silent dedication infectious. On a whim, I even tried the city library and a park during warmer days.

Delving Deeper into the Science:

When we talk about the brain's affinity for novelty, we're diving deep into the realm of neuroscience. Here's a brief on how our grey matter responds to new environments:

- **Novelty and Dopamine:** Every time you expose yourself to a new environment or a new stimulus, your brain releases dopamine, the so-called "feel-good" neurotransmitter. This isn't just about making you feel good; it plays a pivotal role in motivation, memory formation, and information processing. When we're in a new environment, this dopamine release makes us more alert, motivated, and receptive to information.

- **Memory Anchors in Varied Environments:** Our memories are not just about what we learn; they're also about where and when we learn it. That's why you can often recall the café's hum or the park's rustling leaves when thinking about a particular topic. By changing study spots, you give your brain multiple 'contexts' for the same piece of information, making recall more efficient. It's called the "context-dependent memory."

- **Enhanced Creativity:** Different environments expose us to various stimuli. The bustling café may feed your brain ambient conversations, music, or even the scent of freshly baked bread. These stimuli can unconsciously spark connections in your brain, often leading to those 'Eureka!' moments. Ever wondered why some of your best ideas come when you're in the shower or taking a walk? It's the mix of a relaxed state and a different environment.

- **Staving off Mental Fatigue:** Let's face it; long study sessions can be draining. After a while, the brain starts to feel the strain, and our focus dwindles. Changing environments acts as a soft 'reset' button. It's similar to taking a short break but with the added bonus of new stimuli to refresh the mind.

Understanding this science is a game-changer. It's not about hopping from one café to another on a whim; it's about strategically leveraging your brain's inherent mechanisms to optimize learning. It's about working in tandem with your mind, understanding its rhythms, and using them to your advantage.

Making the Most of It:

Variety is the Spice: Don't just rotate between indoor spots. Mix it up. From the vibrant ambiance of a bustling city square to the tranquil sounds at the lakeside, explore diverse environments. And if you're someone who thrives in the hush of a library, maybe try the rooftop terrace of a local building for a change. Or if you've always been a homebody, a quiet corner in your local museum or art gallery could be an untapped reservoir of inspiration.

Engage the Senses: Every locale offers a unique sensory experience. The whiff of old books in a library, the aroma of fresh coffee in a café, the rustling of leaves in a park – let them envelop you. These sensory stimuli not only improve memory anchoring but can also evoke a plethora of emotions, keeping your study sessions emotionally rich and far from monotonous.

People Watch: Occasionally taking your eyes off your notes and observing the world around you can be therapeutic. Watch the barista craft a cappuccino, children playing in the park, or simply the ebb and flow of pedestrians on a sidewalk. It's a subtle reminder that there's a world outside your books, providing tiny mental breaks that can recharge your cognitive batteries.

Stay Unpredictable: The brain loves novelty, remember? So, no strict schedules here. If you went to a café today, maybe hit a botanical garden tomorrow. Or if today was all about indoor studying, make tomorrow about finding a cozy spot under a tree. The unpredictability keeps your brain on its toes, making every study session a mini-adventure.

Optimal Timing: Different places have different peak times. If you love the hum of a café but not the lunchtime rush, time your visits. Similarly, parks might be quieter in the early mornings or late afternoons.

Carry the Essentials: Wherever you go, ensure you have the essentials. A comfortable pair of headphones, a notebook, your study materials, and perhaps a snack. Being prepared helps you settle into your new spot faster.

Feedback Loop: After each session, spend a minute reflecting on how productive it was. Did the park's ambient sounds aid concentration, or were they a distraction? This self-awareness will help you fine-tune your choices in the future.

Remember, the goal is not to turn study sessions into a travel expedition but to find those sweet spots where your brain feels both relaxed and alert. It's about ensuring that every hour spent studying is an hour well spent.

HACK FOUR

The Feynman Technique – Teach to Learn

Alright, gather 'round, fellow knowledge-seekers! Ever heard of the adage, "If you can't explain it to a six-year-old, you don't understand it yourself"? That nugget of wisdom comes from our main man, Einstein. And building on that very principle is the Feynman Technique.

Beth, bustling amidst the majestic buildings of King's College London, was a sharp psychology student. But every so often, she'd hit a conceptual wall. Some topics were like a tangled mess in her mind, with all their intricate details and nuances.

ENTER THE FEYNMAN TECHNIQUE. HERE'S HOW IT ROLLS:

- Simple Language, Always: Imagine explaining your topic to a child. Use basic words, no jargon allowed. If you can't? Well, mate, that's a sign. Dive deeper into your notes.

- The Rating Game: After your 'lesson', rate your understanding out of 10. Got a solid 9 or 10? You're golden. A 5 or 6? That's your brain telling you to revisit certain areas.

- Patch the Gaps: If you faltered or used complex terms, pinpoint the tricky parts. These are your blind spots.

- Re-explain: Armed with a clearer understanding, give it another go. Imagine you're talking to someone with zero knowledge of the topic. Simplify, simplify, simplify.

- Test the Waters: Try teaching different folks. The questions they pose can spotlight areas you hadn't considered and further deepen your understanding.

Beth's Brainwave: Beth took this technique and made it her study mantra. For her, the biggest win was realising that understanding wasn't about fancy words or detailed descriptions. It was about distilling knowledge into its essence. When she ran into a fellow student struggling with a concept, she'd say, "Imagine you had to explain this to a curious ten-year-old. How'd you go about it?"

The results? Mind-blowing. Complex concepts were stripped down to their core, making them easier to grasp and remember.

The science behind this is as straightforward as the technique itself. Our brain, when forced to simplify, delves deeper into the concept. It cuts through the fluff and zeroes in on the heart of the matter. By pretending to teach, you're reinforcing neural pathways, making the info stick.

So, the next time a topic feels like a monstrous, insurmountable mountain, pull out the Feynman Technique. Trust me, you'll not only scale that peak, but you'll also plant a flag on its summit, marking your triumph over the trickiest of topics. And hey, who knows, you might just become the unofficial 'study guru' in your circle!

HACK FIVE

Active Recall – Question Everything

Alright, let's have a chinwag about the big 'A' – Active Recall. Sounds fancy, doesn't it? But strip away the jargon, and it's a straightforward yet killer technique to lodge info deep into the noggin.

Ever been in this boat? You're reading pages of notes, nodding along, thinking, "Yeah, I've got this". Then, when the rubber meets the road (a.k.a. exam time), you draw a massive blank. "But I read all of this!" you wail. That, my friend, is where Active Recall swaggers in to save the day

THE WHY:

See, our brains are a bit cheeky. Just because something's been read doesn't mean it's been retained. You've got to make the grey matter work for its keep! Studies galore have shown that when you actively test yourself, your brain recognises the information as essential. It's like telling your brain, "Oi! Pay attention. This bit's important."

HOW TO SMASH IT:

- Stop and Quiz: After reading a section, close your notes. Now, write down or say out loud everything you remember. Don't peek!
- Flashcards: Old school but gold. On one side, write a question or a keyword. On the other, the answer or a brief explanation. Regularly test yourself. Over time, the answers will come to you as naturally as craving a pizza on a Friday night.
- Teach a Mate: Remember our chat about the Feynman Technique? Double down on it. Get a mate, explain a topic, and then have them throw questions at you. If you can answer on the fly, you're golden. If not, you've got a clear area to brush up on.
- Break It Down: Divide topics into smaller chunks and tackle one chunk at a time. After each, do a quick recall session.

Katie's Recollection Revolution: Katie, a literature major from Sussex, had a stack of poems and prose to memorise. The old Katie would've read them over and over, hoping they'd stick. But post-Active Recall revelation? She'd read a stanza, look away, and try to recite it. Then, she'd jot down the themes or imagery used, without glancing at the text. By exam time, Katie wasn't just regurgitating lines; she was understanding and analysing them on the fly.

Deep Dive Into Science: Now, let's get a tad nerdy. When you employ Active Recall, you're strengthening neural connections. Think of it like hiking. The first time you walk a new trail, it's a bit tough, a tad unclear. But tramp down it repeatedly? You'll carve out a clear, easy-to-navigate path. Similarly, every time you actively recall something, you're reinforcing that neural trail in your brain.

So, next time you're faced with a beast of a topic, don't just passively wade through. Get stuck in, question yourself, and make that information stick. After all, what's the point of learning if you can't remember? And with Active Recall in your toolkit, you won't just remember; you'll own that knowledge.

HACK SIX

Mnemonics and Memory Palaces – Making Memory Fun

Alright, you savvy scholar, ready for another dose of wisdom? Let's get whimsical with mnemonics and morph our minds into grand palaces. If that sounds bonkers, buckle up! You're in for a treat.

The Magic of Mnemonics: First, what's this funky word? Mnemonics (pronounced neh-mon-iks) are just fancy memory aids. Think of them as the brain's equivalent of sticky notes. And these aren't some newfangled gimmicks – they've been around since ancient times!

- Rhyme Time: Who says studying can't be poetic? Transform boring lists into snappy rhymes. For instance, remembering the directions on a compass? "Never Eat Soggy Waffles" (North, East, South, West). Voila! You just made cardinal directions catchy.
- Acronyms and Acrostics: Got a list? Make it an acronym. Take the word HOMES to remember the Great Lakes (Huron, Ontario, Michigan, Erie, Superior). Or how about "Please Excuse My Dear Aunt Sally" for the order of mathematical operations? That's PEMDAS: Parentheses, Exponents, Multiplication and Division, and Addition and Subtraction.

Memory Palaces: A Palace in Your Mind: Imagine walking through your childhood home, placing facts or topics in different rooms. To recall, stroll through the rooms, and the info just pops back!

- Craft Your Palace: Begin with a familiar place - your house, a school, a favourite haunt. It should be somewhere you know inside out.
- Place Your Info: Have a list of things to remember? Place each item in a specific location. If you're studying anatomy, for instance, maybe the skeletal system's in the kitchen (with bones in the cupboard!), and the cardiovascular system's in the living room, with the heart on the couch.

- Walkthrough: When it's crunch time, mentally walk through your palace. As you move from room to room, the placed items (or facts) will spring back to mind.

Meet Archie from Edinburgh: This lad was a history buff, waist-deep in dates and events. Mnemonics became his BFF. For World War I's start in 1914, he'd hum "One-nine, one-four, when the world went to war!" Memory palaces? They were his trick for political treaties. The Treaty of Versailles? He imagined it sitting, all official-like, on his study desk. By exam time, Archie wasn't just recalling; he was recounting tales and dates like a bard!

Diving into Science: Why do these tricks tick? It's all about connections. Our brains adore patterns and stories. By linking dry info to catchy rhymes or vivid locations, we're tapping into the brain's love for narratives. The more vivid and bizarre, the better it sticks!

So, next time you're staring down a hefty chunk of info, give these techniques a whirl. Turn learning from a chore into a delightful journey, where your brain's the hero, conquering facts with flair!

05 Chapter 5 - Social Life and Networking

Pull up a chair, you social butterfly in the making! We're diving deep into the art of jiving, jiggling, and just plain jamming with the best of them. Whether you're the life of the party or the wallflower quietly observing, there's a trick or two up our sleeves to get you rubbing shoulders, exchanging business cards (or Insta handles, more likely), and getting the most out of uni social life. Because let's face it: while that degree's top-notch, the friends, memories, and connections you make along the way? Priceless.

HACK ONE Join the Club – Societies and You

Alright, let's keep it a hundred here: Unis can be both exciting and a tad overwhelming, right? Thousands of students, everyone rushing around, and it can sometimes feel like everyone's found their 'tribe' except you. Now, what if I told you there's a shortcut to finding your kind of people? Enter: societies.

Why Societies?
You see, societies aren't just some posh word for clubs. They're like the backstage pass to the rock concert that is uni life. Big into films? There's probably a society for that. Got a thing for baking? Bet there's a society whipping up some goodies right now. And the magic of it? Everyone's there because they love it. Instant common ground.

A Few Tips to Navigate the Society Scene:
- Fresher's Fair: Think of this as the Black Friday of society sign-ups. There's a buzz in the air, lots of freebies, and tons of enthusiasm. Our mate Liam from Glasgow? He signed up for the Anime Society on a whim, and now he's the president. Go figure!

- **Trial Sessions:** Most societies get it; commitment can be scary. That's why they have these 'come and see if you like it' sessions. It's like test-driving a car. Sarah from Leeds tried out three different societies before settling on the Dance Society. She went for the salsa, stayed for the people (and the moves!).

- **Lead the Pack:** Maybe you've got a unique hobby. Like, I dunno, underwater basket weaving? If there isn't already a society for it, roll up those sleeves and start one. Josh from Cardiff did just that with his passion for drone racing. And guess what? It's now one of the hottest societies on campus!

Breaking the 'Uncool' Myth:

Okay, time to address the elephant in the room. Some folks think joining a society might be a bit... nerdy? But here's the tea: societies are basically the uni equivalent of joining a band. Remember Alex from Manchester? People raised eyebrows when he joined the Harry Potter Society. Fast forward to now, and those same folks are begging him for tickets to the annual Yule Ball event.

In a nutshell? Societies aren't just clubs. They're your ticket to fast friendships, mad experiences, and some killer stories for those nights out. Dive in, be genuine, and let the good times roll!

HACK TWO
Mastering the Mix – Perfecting the Art of Mingling

Right, let's dive straight into it. You're at an event, clutching a drink, and suddenly that all-familiar wave of dread washes over you. People are chatting away, the room's abuzz, and you're rooted to the spot, wondering how to dive into the whirlpool without drowning. Yep, we're talking about the age-old skill of mingling. But here's a secret: It's less about the words and more about the vibe. Let's break it down.

Why Even Bother Mingling?

Because life, especially at uni, is more than just grades and classes. It's the connections, the experiences, the shared moments. Plus, being able to comfortably chat with strangers? That's a superpower that can elevate your game, both in the social and professional arenas.

Confidence is Your Secret Weapon:

Before we even get to the tips, here's the foundation: confidence. Now, don't roll your eyes! I ain't talking about swaggering into a room like you own the joint. It's about being comfortable in your skin. Remember Ellie from University of Bristol? She was shy, quiet, the typical wallflower. But over time, she realised confidence isn't about volume; it's about authenticity. She started attending events, not with the mindset to impress, but to express. The change? Night and day.

Now, For the Tips:

- Your Vibe Attracts Your Tribe: Before you walk into an event, take a moment. Deep breath. Remind yourself: You're not here to win anyone over. You're here to meet, interact, and perhaps, make a few memories.
- Body Language Speaks: Stand open, not closed off. Make eye contact. Smile. These little tweaks don't just make you seem approachable; they actually make you FEEL more open to conversations.
- Shared Experiences are Gold: Look around. Is there something peculiar about the venue? Maybe a quirky painting, or perhaps the DJ's playing an absolute banger? Comment on it. Shared experiences are instant icebreakers.
- Celebrate Others: Met someone who's doing something cool? Celebrate it. A genuine compliment or show of interest can kickstart the most memorable of interactions.
- And If All Else Fails... Remember, you're in a room full of potential friends, not judges. If a conversation's going south, no stress! Gracefully exit and move on. There are plenty of chats in the sea.

HACK THREE

Stay in the Loop – Never Miss an Event

Alright, party animals and social butterflies, this one's for you. But also for the introverts and the 'maybe I'll go, maybe I won't' folks. Because let's face it, nothing stings quite like the pang of regret when you hear tales of that epic night out or that chilled movie night you missed. FOMO (Fear Of Missing Out) isn't just a millennial catchphrase; it's the uni student's silent nemesis.

Let's tackle it, shall we?
Why Stay in the Loop?

University life is a blend of highs and lows, studies and parties, and, quite simply, moments that make for stories you'll recount for years to come. Missed opportunities often morph into 'what ifs'. So, how do you ensure you're at the right place at the right time?

The Golden Rules to Staying Updated:

- University Socials - Your Event Diary: Every uni's got its official (and some not-so-official) social media channels. These are treasure troves of event announcements, updates, and reminders. From guest lectures to surprise DJ nights, if it's happening, it's likely on here. Set notifications, or better yet, bookmark them.

- The Mighty Group Chats: Before you groan and think of the endless notifications, hear me out. Whether it's WhatsApp or Telegram, group chats often are where plans are birthed. From a spontaneous trip to the beach to that study group you absolutely need before finals, being active (or at least not muting every single chat) can be a game-changer.

- **Old School Still Rocks – Bulletin Boards:** In our digital age, it's easy to dismiss these wooden boards peppered with flyers as relics. But many a time, these boards flaunt some of the most unique local events. Jazz nights, poetry slams, or that indie band that's just too underground for mainstream channels – bulletin boards have your back.

- **Be Proactive:** If you're passionate about something, why wait? Seek out related societies or groups. Music lover? There's probably a club for that. Into drama? Join the theatre group. This ensures you're the first to know (and sometimes, even organise) related events.

- **Networking with Seniors:** Chatting with students from higher years can be enlightening. They've been in the loop longer and can give you the lowdown on events that might not be as heavily advertised but are absolute must-attends.

In the whirlwind of university life, it's easy to feel overwhelmed or out of touch. But by staying in the loop, you not only open doors to socialising and networking but also to experiences that might just end up defining your university journey. So, next time an event pops up, maybe give it a go? You never know where it might lead.

HACK FOUR

Your Home Away from Home – Local Pubs and Spots

Gather round, you eager beavers! We've all heard the tales of that quirky local pub or coffee shop which becomes a student's second home during their uni years. Not just for the drinks or the food, but for the warmth, camaraderie, and the sheer experience of it. And while you might have visions of your mate Dave doing a somewhat questionable rendition of "Wonderwall" on karaoke night, these spots are about so much more.

Why the Local Dive?

Sure, your university campus might have a buzzing nightlife and plenty of events. But stepping out of that bubble and into the local scene can offer a completely different experience. It's where the town and the gown merge, where you meet locals who've lived in the city for years and have stories that pre-date your fresher's week fiascos.

Maximising the Local Experience:

- **Weekly Quizzes – Engage those Brain Cells:** Nothing screams 'British pub' more than a good old pub quiz. This isn't just about flaunting your trivia prowess, though that's a perk. It's about teaming up, strategising, and sometimes laughing at just how much (or how little) you all know. Plus, there's usually a prize involved. Free pints, anyone?

- **Theme Nights – There's One for Everyone:** No matter your musical taste or preferred dance style, local spots have got you covered. Swing by on jazz night, sing your heart out on karaoke evenings or discover local bands on indie nights. Each event is a new chance to meet like-minded people and bond over shared interests.

- **The Old-Timers – A Goldmine of Wisdom:** Every local joint has them. The regulars who've seen students come and go, who've probably been patrons since before you were born. They're fonts of local history and legends. Chatting with them can give you a unique perspective on the place you're studying in. And who knows, maybe you'll pick up a life lesson or two over a pint.

- **Discounts and Deals:** Student night or special discounts for uni folk? Many local spots offer these to attract the younger crowd. Keep an eye out, and you might save a quid or two.

- **Networking Opportunities:** You'd be surprised how many informal job opportunities or internships arise from casual pub conversations. Maybe the regular sitting next to you knows someone who knows someone. In the professional world, connections matter.
- **Become a Regular:** There's something comforting about walking into a place where the bartender knows your usual order. Regulars often get the best seats, the latest gossip, and occasionally, a drink on the house.

So, next time you're thinking of a night out, maybe skip that overcrowded student bar and head to a local haunt. It could be the start of some of your best uni memories. And Dave? Maybe with enough practice, he'll nail that "Wonderwall" cover after all. Cheers!

HACK FIVE

Cultivate Genuine Connections – Beyond the Initial Chat

Alright, legends, here's a real tea-spiller for you. We've all been there: meeting scores of new faces at the start of the term, exchanging names, courses, hometowns - the usual drill. But let's be real for a sec. How many of those 'Hi, nice to meet you' encounters actually transition to 'Mate, remember that insane night?' memories? Not too many, right? Let's change that.

Why Dive Deeper?

University is a massive melting pot of personalities, stories, and backgrounds. But while it's easy to float on the surface, the true treasures lie in the depths. It's about those 2 AM heart-to-hearts, those shared laughs over inside jokes, those shoulders to cry on when the going gets tough. Quantity is cool for Insta followers, but in real life? Quality wins every time.

Solidifying those Fresh Connections:

- **Coffee Connects People:** Picture this. You're leaving a lecture, and you find yourself walking in the same direction as someone from your course. Instead of the typical small talk about how tedious the lecture was, shoot your shot: "Fancy grabbing a coffee?" It's simple, spontaneous, and guess what? It works. Our very own author swears by this tactic. It's how he went from nodding acquaintances with course mates to having deep discussions about life, the universe, and the perplexing nature of certain lecturers' handwriting.

- **Follow-ups are Your Best Mates:** So, you've had a good chat with someone at a party or during a group project. Great start! But, what next? A simple message like "Hey, really enjoyed our chat yesterday. Fancy a round of drinks this weekend?" can turn a fleeting interaction into a budding friendship.

- **Genuine Interest is Gold**: Remember little things. Did someone mention they had a big presentation or an important game coming up? Ask them how it went the next time you bump into them. It shows you care.

- **Bring 'em into the Fold:** Met someone you click with? Invite them over to a movie night with your mates or a casual dinner. Shared experiences fast-track friendships.

With these hacks under your belt, you'll go from being 'that person I met once' to 'the mate I can't imagine uni without'. Dive deep, make those connections count, and treasure the memories you create.

06 Chapter 6 - The Hangovers

Hangover Havens: Navigating the Aftermath of a Legendary Night Out

Alright, you legends. Before we delve deep into the life-saving hacks, we've got to understand the beast we're dealing with. Ever wondered why after a night of revelry, the morning feels like a cruel joke played by the universe? Let's dissect this infamous state we call a hangover. Knowledge is power, after all!

1. The Hangover Anatomy: What's Going On?

A. The Brain Boogie: When you're sipping on that vodka cranberry or downing a pint, alcohol is busy at work in your brain. It messes with the neurotransmitters, chemicals that regulate our mood. Initially, you feel euphoric, invincible even. But as the alcohol levels drop, so does the feel-good neurotransmitter levels, leading to that dreaded hangover gloom.

B. The Sahara Desert Effect: Ever felt like you've crossed the desert without a drop of water post-night-out? Alcohol is a diuretic. This means it makes you pee more. While you're busy belting out tunes and breaking moves on the dance floor, you're also losing fluids, leading to dehydration. This loss of fluids results in that pounding headache and Sahara-dry mouth.

C. Tummy Turmoil: That rumbling in your tummy isn't just from the dodgy kebab. Alcohol irritates the stomach lining, increases acid production, and slows down the rate at which the stomach empties itself. This trio of terror leads to nausea and sometimes, that dreaded rush to the bathroom.

D. The Sleep Sham: You'd think after passing out for hours, you'd wake up refreshed. Alas, not the case! Alcohol can send you to sleep swiftly but it plays havoc with your REM (Rapid Eye Movement) cycle. This means that even though you're out cold, you're not getting the deep, restorative sleep your body craves.

2. The Culprits Behind the Curtain: What's Causing It?

A. Quantity, Quantity, Quantity: The more you drink, the worse the hangover. It's a simple equation. Downing a drink or two might leave you merry, but several more? That's when the hangover ogre really strikes.

B. Dark vs Light: Dark drinks like red wine, brandy, and certain whiskeys contain congeners. These are toxic chemicals that arise during the fermentation process. They can exacerbate hangovers, so it's often better to stick with clearer drinks if you're looking to sidestep the post-party blues.

C. Mixing the Potion: Ever heard the saying, "Beer before wine, you'll feel fine. Wine before beer, you'll feel queer"? Mixing your drinks can be a one-way ticket to hangover hell. Your body doesn't appreciate the cocktail chaos!

3. It's Not Just the Booze: Other Factors at Play

A. Lack of Food: Ah, the ol' "drinking on an empty stomach" routine. Picture this: your stomach, a bit like a sponge, is ready and raring to soak up anything you pour into it. Now, when you've had a decent meal, the stomach takes its sweet time absorbing the alcohol, releasing it slowly into your bloodstream. But on an empty stomach? That alcohol floods in like a tidal wave, causing blood alcohol concentration to spike swiftly. This can intensify alcohol's effects on your body and mind, making you feel tipsy faster and also amplifying the after-effects the next morning. It's a bit like trying to run a marathon without any training – you're simply not prepared!

B. Lack of Rest: We've all been there. Dancing the night away, chatting till the wee hours, and then attempting to power through the next day. The catch? Your body operates like a rechargeable battery. Miss out on those golden hours of rest, and it doesn't fully charge. Combine this with alcohol's merry dance in your system, and you're setting the stage for a monstrous hangover. Adequate rest allows your body to heal, regenerate, and process toxins. Skimp on that, and you're essentially asking your body to fight the hangover ogre with one hand tied behind its back.

C. Your Genetic Make-up: Blame it on the DNA! Research has shown that certain genetic factors can influence how our bodies metabolise alcohol. Some of us, thanks to our genetic code, might produce fewer enzymes needed to break down alcohol. This means alcohol and its toxic by-products linger longer in the system, giving rise to more pronounced hangover symptoms.

Think of it as a traffic jam in your system where alcohol is the unruly driver refusing to move on. So, if you've ever wondered why your mate Dave can down pints and feel chirpy the next morning, while you're nursing a throbbing head after just a couple – it could very well be down to your genes.

D. Other Sneaky Culprits:

- Medications: Some prescription or over-the-counter meds can interact with alcohol, intensifying its effects or causing adverse reactions.

- Your Health Status: Chronic conditions or even short-term illnesses can make your body more vulnerable to hangovers. Your body is already working overtime, and alcohol just adds to its workload.

Alright, champs, now that we've taken a deep dive into the murky waters of the hangover, buckle up for the next chapter. We're about to unveil the ultimate toolkit to help you bounce back from even the most legendary of nights out!

HACK ONE

Mastering the Art of Rehydration: No More Parched Mornings!

Alright, folks, gather 'round. If hangovers were a villain in a movie, dehydration would be their sinister sidekick. Why, you ask? Because alcohol is a bit sneaky, encouraging your kidneys to work overtime and forcing you to run to the loo more often than you'd want. And, as our brains are basically like spongy water balloons, the effects of dehydration can lead to that iconic hangover headache. But fear not, we've got the hydration hacks to drench that dry mouth and revitalize your weary body.

1. The Morning Elixir: Water with a Twist We all know water's the first go-to, but let's jazz it up a bit. Start your morning with a tall glass of water spiked with a pinch of Himalayan pink salt and a squeeze of lemon. This isn't just to make your water fancy; it's about replenishing the electrolytes and giving your body a quick vitamin C boost.

2. Herbal Infusions to the Rescue: Consider opting for herbal teas like ginger or chamomile. Not only do they rehydrate, but they also soothe an upset stomach and calm those hangover jitters. Pro tip: Prep a flask before your night out, and it'll be waiting to comfort you come morning.

3. Coconut Water: Nature's Sports Drink Before you reach for that sugary sports drink, crack open a coconut water. It's packed with electrolytes like potassium, which will help recharge your system. Plus, it's a touch sweet, making it a delightful post-night-out pick-me-up.

4. Hydration Snacks: Yes, You Can Eat Your Water! Let's get munching on water-rich foods. Think watermelon, strawberries, or cucumber slices sprinkled with a dash of salt. These snacks pack a double punch – they'll quench your thirst and satisfy those post-drinking munchies.

5. Fizzy Saviour: Sparkling Water Sometimes, plain ol' water doesn't cut it. Enter sparkling water! It offers a refreshing change with its fizzy bubbles. Add a splash of fruit juice or a slice of citrus to ramp up the flavour. But avoid the sugary sodas; they might seem tempting, but they're no friends of hydration.

6. The Broth Bowl: Got a pot of broth or a pack of miso soup lying around? Heat it up! Not only will the warm liquid soothe your insides, but broths are also rich in salts and other nutrients that your body might be craving after a wild night.

7. Water Schedule: If your hangover has left you a bit dazed, set a reminder on your phone to drink water every 20 minutes. It might seem over the top, but trust us, your body will thank you later.

8. DIY Hydration Popsicles: For those days when the thought of drinking anything might make you queasy, have some homemade hydration popsicles on standby. Mix some fruit juice (think orange or pineapple) with water, pour into moulds, and freeze. These icy delights can be a lifesaver on a rough morning.

There you have it, hydration warriors! Remember, while it's essential to quench that thirst, pace yourself. Too much water too quickly might not sit well with a fragile stomach. Intersperse these hacks throughout your day, and you'll be back to your dazzling self in no time.

HACK TWO

Carb Loading: Fuel Up & Fight the Hangover Haze

Alright, my hungover comrades! Ever woken up from a night of shenanigans feeling like you've been hit by a double-decker bus from York Uni's main campus? That grogginess you feel might be your brain throwing a little tantrum because it's running on empty. Yep, our noggins love carbs, especially when we've been throwing back a pint (or three). But before you go scoffing down a greasy fry-up, let's look at smarter ways to reintroduce those essential carbs into your system.

1. The Humble Toast: Not Just Bread, But a Lifesaver Bread gets a bad rep these days, but a slice of whole grain toast is your morning-after bestie. It offers a steady release of energy, preventing any sudden spikes or crashes in your blood sugar levels. Plus, it's gentle on the stomach. Upgrade your slice with a smear of honey or jam for that extra bit of sugar goodness.

2. Bananas: Nature's Energy Bar Nature's wrapped up a perfect dose of carbs, vitamins, and minerals in a handy yellow package. Bananas have potassium, which is great for replenishing those electrolytes you lost while showing off your dance moves.

3. Oatmeal or Porridge: The Ultimate Comfort Bowl A hot, creamy bowl of oats isn't just winter comfort food; it's the ideal post-night-out recovery meal. Oats release energy slowly, ensuring your blood sugar levels stay stable. Toss in some berries or a spoon of maple syrup to sweeten the deal.

4. Rice Cakes: Lightweight and Mighty If the idea of heavy food makes you queasy, rice cakes are a top choice. They're light, airy, and can be topped with almost anything, from peanut butter to avocado, giving you a carb boost without weighing you down.

5. Fruit Juice: A Sugary Sip While you're hydrating, why not add a touch of natural sugar to the mix? Orange, apple, or even pineapple juice can offer a quick pick-me-up, giving your brain that much-needed glucose to get back on track.

6. Smoothies: When Chewing Feels Overrated For those mornings when the thought of eating is too much, blend up a smoothie. A mix of yoghurt, fruits, and maybe a hint of honey or maple syrup can offer both hydration and energy in one go.

7. Energy Balls: Bite-sized Powerhouses Prep some energy balls made of dates, nuts, and oats during your sober days, and you'll thank your past self when the hangover hits. They're small, packed with carbs, and require minimal effort to consume.

8. Plain Crackers or Biscuits: Simple yet Effective Sometimes, simplicity is best. Plain crackers or digestives can gently reintroduce carbs without overwhelming a sensitive stomach.

When your night out drains your body's fuel reserves, carbs come to the rescue. Remember, though, it's all about balance. The aim is to gently elevate your blood sugar levels without causing any sudden spikes. So, the next time you wake up feeling a tad worse for wear, reach out for one of these carb solutions, and watch the hangover clouds lift.

Ready for more pearls of wisdom to conquer those nasty hangovers? Stick around, because we've got more solid gold advice in the pipeline!

HACK THREE

Clear Skies Ahead - Why You Might Want to Rethink that Dark Drink

Oi, you party animal! Ever noticed how some nights leave you in the hangover trenches, while others have you bouncing back like you've had ten hours of kip? It might have something to do with the type of drink you're dancing with.

Let's dive deep into the mysterious world of drinks and their colours, and why choosing clear might just be the ticket to waking up fresher than a daisy in York's springtime!

1. Understanding the Culprit: Enter Congeners First off, what the blazes are congeners? Well, these cheeky little compounds are by-products of the fermentation and distillation processes in booze. While they can add flavour and depth, they're also masterminds behind intensifying your hangovers. Darker drinks pack more congeners than their clear counterparts. The darker the drink, the heavier the hangover weight.

2. The Dark Side: Whiskey, Red Wine & Tequila While sipping on a fine aged whiskey or savouring a deep red wine sounds like the sophisticated choice, they come with a caveat. These beverages might have more flavour nuances (thanks to congeners), but they're also more likely to make you feel like you've been run over by the morning bus. And tequila? It might lead to some epic dance moves, but those moves might be followed by an epic headache.

3. Clear Choice Heroes: Vodka & Gin Swapping to clear spirits like vodka and gin could be your ticket to a smoother morning. They're distilled more times, which means fewer congeners. Plus, let's be real – a well-mixed gin and tonic or a vodka soda with a splash of lime can be equally delightful on a night out.

4. Methanol Madness : Here's a nifty bit of science for you. Among those pesky congeners is methanol. When our bodies break down methanol, it results in formaldehyde and formic acid – two compounds that don't play nice. They're a big part of the reason why you feel like your head's in a vice after indulging in dark drinks.

5. Mixing Matters : Ever heard the saying, "Beer before liquor, never been sicker; liquor before beer, you're in the clear"? There might be some truth behind the rhyme. Mixing drinks can mess with your system and intensify a hangover. If you do switch, try moving from dark to clear to reduce those nasty morning-after effects.

If you fancy a tipple, considering the colour might just save your bacon the next day. By no means are we saying ditch your beloved red wine or whiskey forever, but if you've got a big day ahead, opting for something clearer might be a good shout. Remember, it's all about enjoying responsibly, staying hydrated, and finding the drink that suits both your palate and your morning.

HACK FOUR

Picking Your Pills - Navigating Pain Relief After a Tipple

Alright, party warriors of York University! So you've had a blinder of a night, but now your head feels like it's hosting a solo drum gig. You're rummaging through your medicine drawer for a quick fix, but WAIT! Not all painkillers play nice with the remnants of last night's mischief.

Let's have a chinwag about which tablets might help you recover, and which ones to swerve if you don't want to feel even rougher.

1. The Go-To's: Aspirin and Ibuprofen Both aspirin and ibuprofen fall under the umbrella of nonsteroidal anti-inflammatory drugs (or NSAIDs for short). These bad boys can be real lifesavers when it comes to battling that nasty hangover headache.

- **Aspirin:** This old-school remedy can help ease the pounding in your noggin. It's an anti-inflammatory, so it can tackle those aches and pains post-night-out. However, if your stomach's feeling a bit iffy after all those pints, be cautious. Aspirin can be a tad harsh on an empty or alcohol-irritated stomach.

- **Ibuprofen (Nurofen, for the Brits out there):** Another champion in the pain relief game. Like aspirin, it can combat inflammation, making it a top choice for battling that post-booze body ache. Just a word of warning: same as aspirin, it can be a bit of a troublemaker if your stomach's on the sensitive side.

2. Steer Clear of Acetaminophen (Paracetamol in the UK) Now, you might be thinking: "Why not just pop a couple of Paracetamol?" It's a common remedy for headaches and pains, right? Well, here's the rub: if there's still a bit of alcohol swimming about in your system, mixing it with Paracetamol can be a recipe for trouble. This combo can amplify the potential toxic effects on your liver, and trust us, you don't want to add that to your list of problems.

3. Always Read the Label Here's a golden nugget of wisdom: always, ALWAYS read the label before taking any medication. If you're on any other meds or have underlying health conditions, it's crucial to ensure that you're not mixing something that could land you in hot water.

While painkillers can be a blessing for those horrid hangover headaches, it's crucial to make an informed choice. Look after your noggin and your liver by picking the right pill. And remember, the best remedy is always prevention: drink water, pace yourself, and enjoy responsibly.

HACK FIVE

Java Jolt - The Coffee Chronicles

Alright, all you lovely lads and lasses, if you've ever reached out for a cuppa joe after a wild night, you might just be onto something. Let's brew some facts, shall we?

1. Coffee: Not Just Your Morning Wake-Up Call The humble coffee, a student staple, isn't just to get you through those dreary morning lectures. That caffeine kick can help combat the grogginess that feels like you've been dragged through a hedge backward after a night on the tiles.

2. Caffeine: The Alertness Alchemist Caffeine acts as a stimulant. Now, what does that mean for your tired noggin? It nudges your central nervous system, helping you feel more awake and alert. So, while it might not directly battle the hangover demons, it sure does give you a leg up against that drowsy feeling.

3. But Beware The Mix: Now, before you start downing espresso shots with your evening pint – hold your horses! Mixing alcohol and caffeine can be like oil and water. Here's the tricky bit: caffeine can mask some depressant effects of alcohol. That's right, it can make you feel more sober than you actually are, potentially leading you to drink more. A risky game!

4. Not Just Coffee: If you're not one for the bitterness of a black coffee, fear not. Tea, with its gentler caffeine content, can also be your ally. Green tea, especially, comes packed with antioxidants, which can be just the ticket to help your liver along after its marathon of processing all that booze.

5. Moderation is Key: Like all good things, the trick is not to overdo it. Too much caffeine can make you jittery, increase heart rate, or even worsen that hangover headache. So, while a cup or two might be golden, guzzling down a whole pot? Maybe not the brightest bulb in the box.

HACK SIX

Boosting with B Vitamins & Zippy Zinc

Hey, party people! So, ever wondered why some of your pals bounce back after a night out while others (possibly you) are draped over the sofa regretting those last couple of drinks? The answer could lie in B vitamins and zinc. Let's dive in.
The B-Team:

Imagine B vitamins as the backstage crew at a concert. You don't always see them, but they're making sure everything runs smoothly. Alcohol, that raucous headliner, can shove these unsung heroes out of the way, leading to the dreaded hangover encore.
Zinc on the Beat:

Enter Zinc: the sturdy roadie of the mineral world, ensuring everything is in its right place. It's involved in countless bodily reactions, including helping break down our drinks of choice. More zinc might mean less morning-after drama.

Study Breakdown:
Science moment: A nibble of research from The Journal of Clinical Medicine threw these two into the spotlight. People who'd been munching on foods rich in B vitamins and zinc just seemed to handle their hangovers better. But remember, it's a small-scale study, so it's like basing a restaurant review on one bite of a starter.

Foodie Fix:
Think of loading up on these nutrients as pre-party prep. Legumes, grains, nuts, seeds - it's not just health jargon, it's your party recovery kit. Imagine a pre-night-out ritual: A hearty bowl of chickpea curry or a zinc-rich pumpkin seed snack. It's like putting on armour before the battle.

Pill or Plate:
If you're considering supplements, picture them as the VIP pass to the nutrition gig. They're handy, but they don't replace the real experience. It's always a good shout to chat with a healthcare expert before jumping on the supplement bandwagon.

So, there you have it! While we can't promise a hangover-free experience, arming yourself with B vitamins and zinc might give you a fighting chance. Prep, party, recover, repeat!

So to wrap up!

How to Sidestep Those Sneaky Hangovers

1. Pace Yourself, Maverick:
Remember that childhood game, "The Tortoise and the Hare"? Be the tortoise. Enjoy your drink, sip by sip, rather than downing it in one go. Why rush when you've got all night?

2. Fill 'er Up (Your Stomach, That Is):
Always, and I mean always, team up your drink with some grub. Think of it as your booze buffer. It slows down the absorption, giving you a smoother sail.

3. Play By The Rules:
Yeah, rules might sound a bit schoolyard, but they're kinda handy. For the ladies, aim for no more than a drink a day, and for the gents, cap it at two. What's in a drink? About a pint of beer, a small glass of vino, or a shot of your fave spirit. But hey, we get it. Some nights are wilder than others. Just know your limits and play it cool.

4. Hydrate to Dominate:
Booze has a sneaky way of sapping your hydration superpowers. Every time you down a drink, chase it with a glass of water. Not only will it help dilute the alcohol, but it'll also combat that pesky dehydration. Plus, it's a great way to pace yourself!

5. The Final Word:
We all love a good party, and sometimes we go a bit overboard. No judgements here! But if tomorrow's a big day and you can't afford to be in zombie mode, stick to the playbook. You'll thank yourself in the morning.

07 Chapter 7 - Health and Wellbeing

Alright, mates, gather 'round! Let's have a chinwag about something a wee bit more serious but oh-so-crucial: Your health and wellbeing. Now, I know, I know. Uni life's all about soaking in new experiences – cramming the night away for that pesky exam, or dancing 'til dawn at the local club. But here's the kicker: How do you reckon you'll do all that if you're feeling knackered or down in the dumps?

Nah, this isn't a lecture about munching on kale or meditating atop a Himalayan peak. It's about practical, doable hacks that ensure you're not just living the student life but thriving through it. Want to find out how to nail that perfect balance of kebabs and cardio? Or perhaps manage those stress gremlins that pop up during exam season? Dive in, and let's get you sorted, from noggin to toes, ensuring you're in the prime of health to tackle anything uni throws at you! Let's get cracking!

HACK ONE   Fueling the Machine

Alright, settle in folks. Let's chat about our mate Connor. First-year at uni, a bit lost in the whirlwind of new experiences, and yeah, surviving mostly on takeaways and those oh-so-tempting late-night kebabs. The result? Sluggish mornings, foggy thinking, and a waistline that was expanding faster than his lecture notes.

But, a few months in, something clicked for Connor. Maybe it was that breathless race for the bus or the third all-nighter in a row fueled by crisps and energy drinks. He realised he needed to change.

Balanced Diet = Balanced Life: Connor did a bit of digging. A balanced diet wasn't just about looking good; it was about feeling good. Armed with this knowledge, he revamped his food habits. Yes, those pizzas and burgers still made an occasional appearance, but veggies, fruits, lean meats, and whole grains began to dominate his plate. The difference? Clearer skin, more energy, and yep, a sharper mind during those 9 am lectures.

Simple Meal Preps, Big Changes: Being a typical student, Connor didn't fancy spending hours in the kitchen. So, he went for simple meal preps.
- Batch Cooking: Connor started cooking in bulk on Sundays. Chilis, stir-fries, pasta sauces – all portioned out and frozen for the week ahead.
- Overnight Oats: Breakfast transformed from sugary cereals to hearty jars of overnight oats, topped with whatever fruits were on sale that week.
- Wraps Galore: Lunches turned fun with wraps. Grilled chicken, leftover veggies, some hummus, and Connor had a meal that was the envy of his mates.

Budgeting and Bites: On a student budget, Connor had to be savvy.

- Market Hunts: Evening trips to the local market became routine. Those end-of-day discounts on fresh produce? Gold.
- Generic for the Win: Swapping out name brands for store-brand goods saved him a pretty penny without skimping on quality.
- Bulk Buys: Connor started buying essentials like rice and pasta in bulk. A little investment upfront, but savings in the long run.
- Seasonal Choices: He started focusing on in-season produce. Not only cheaper but oh-so-flavourful!

Connor's journey wasn't just about trimming the waist or saving a few quid. It was transformative. As he started fueling his body right, everything shifted – better grades, improved mood, and a newfound zest for life.

His story is a testament: what we put on our plate directly reflects in our day-to-day life. So, taking a leaf out of Connor's book – when it comes to food, make choices that fuel your ambition, not ones that fog your journey.

HACK TWO

From Sedentary to Sprinter – Lily's Fitness Glow-Up

Picture this: Lily, a second-year at Durham. Bright, brilliant, and utterly besotted with her YouTube channel, where she documented her uni life. But between filming, editing, and hunkering down for assignments, Lily was leading a sedentary lifestyle. Hours would zoom by with her glued to her chair, editing clips or typing away.

But, as the weeks turned into months, Lily began feeling the effects. Tight muscles, sporadic sleep patterns, and a general sense of sluggishness. She realised she needed to shake things up, but how? Joining a gym seemed daunting, not to mention expensive. And running? Let's just say she wasn't ready to sprint just yet.

Starting Small: Lily didn't dive headfirst into the deep end. Instead, she dipped her toes in the shallow end. She began with simple stretches every morning. Just 10 minutes to wake her muscles up. Next came desk exercises. Leg lifts, seated marching – small movements but with a big impact.

YouTube to the Rescue: Being the YouTuber she was, Lily decided to explore fitness channels. She stumbled upon short, effective workouts – perfect for her packed schedule.

- <u>HIIT Sessions:</u> High-intensity interval training became her go-to. Quick, 15-minute bursts that got her heart racing and muscles burning.
- <u>Yoga Flow:</u> On days she felt particularly tense, Lily turned to yoga. It helped stretch out those editing-induced kinks and also provided a sense of calm.
- <u>Dance Breaks:</u> Who said workouts couldn't be fun? Every now and then, Lily would blast her favourite tunes and have a mini dance party. A joyful way to get moving!

Incorporating Movement into Daily Life: Lily didn't stop at structured workouts. She found ways to embed movement into her everyday routine.

- <u>Walk and Talk:</u> Instead of sitting for phone calls, she started walking. Catching up with mates while getting her steps in.
- <u>Study Breaks:</u> Every hour of studying was punctuated with a 5-minute movement break. Be it squats or just pacing around her room.
- <u>Take the Stairs:</u> Lily made it a rule. No lifts. Stairs became her mini cardio session.

The results? Within weeks, Lily felt a transformation. Her energy levels soared, sleep improved, and those tight muscles? A thing of the past. But the best part? Her viewers started noticing. Comments poured in, praising her radiant glow and asking for her fitness secrets.

Lily's journey was a testament to the fact that exercise isn't one-size-fits-all. It's about finding what fits into your lifestyle and enjoying the process. As Lily showed, a little can indeed go a long way. Whether you're a budding YouTuber or just someone juggling assignments, remember: every bit of movement counts. So, find your rhythm and dance (or jog, or stretch) your way to a healthier you!

HACK THREE
Brain Breaks - Rethinking Rest for Peak Performance

Enter Chris, a meticulous third-year physics student at the University of Edinburgh. His days? Brimming with equations, labs, and lengthy lectures. Now, Chris was no stranger to pulling all-nighters, chugging coffee, and pushing through brain fog to meet his deadlines. After all, he believed that's what it took to be top of the class.

However, during a particularly intense revision session, Chris had an epiphany. His brain felt like a computer with too many tabs open. It was slowing down, lagging, and close to crashing. The relentless cycle of study, caffeine, repeat wasn't sustainable.

The Power of Pausing: Chris began diving into cognitive science and discovered the potent power of breaks. The brain, it turns out, isn't designed for marathon sessions. It thrives on intervals: focused work followed by dedicated rest.

Quick Techniques for Mental Refresh:

- The 20-20-20 Rule: Every 20 minutes, look at something 20 feet away for at least 20 seconds. This simple technique, primarily for those glued to screens, reduces eye strain and provides a quick cognitive breather.
- Mini Meditation: Not the hour-long Zen sessions. Just 3-5 minutes of focused breathing. Chris would set a timer, close his eyes, and concentrate on his breath. These pockets of calm amidst chaos did wonders for his mental clarity.
- Physical Movement: Every hour, Chris would do a quick physical activity. Be it a set of jumping jacks, a stretch, or a walk around his room. The blood flow wasn't just good for the body but also for the brain.

Sleep: The Unsung Hero: Chris's research led him to another revelation: sleep. Not just the number of hours, but the quality. Sleep was the ultimate brain break. It was when the brain processed information, formed memories, and essentially 'cleaned house'.

He started maintaining a regular sleep schedule, even during heavy revision periods. He also incorporated habits like reducing screen time before bed and keeping his room dark and cool. The result? Waking up feeling genuinely refreshed and having far more productive study sessions.

By semester's end, Chris wasn't just performing better academically; he felt genuinely better. Gone were the days of dragging himself through the week, waiting for the weekend to crash. He had energy, enthusiasm, and, surprisingly, more free time. All because he learned the art of the brain break.

Chris's story drives home a profound truth: In our quest for productivity, we often neglect rest. But, as counterintuitive as it might seem, sometimes the best way to move forward is to take a step back, breathe, and give our brain the break it not just needs but deserves.

- **Sleep Consistency:** Go to bed and wake up at the same time every day, even on weekends. This helps regulate your body's internal clock and improve the quality of your sleep.
- **Sleep Environment:** Make your bedroom conducive to sleep. This includes a comfortable mattress and pillows, blackout curtains to keep the room dark, and using white noise machines or earplugs to block out disruptive sounds.
- **Limit Screen Time:** The blue light emitted by screens on mobile phones, computers, tablets, and televisions restrains the production of melatonin, the hormone responsible for sleep. Try to avoid screens at least an hour before bedtime.
- **Mindful Eating:** Avoid large meals, caffeine, and alcohol before bedtime. They can disrupt sleep and cause discomfort from indigestion.
- **Physical Activity:** Regular physical activity can help regulate your sleep patterns. However, avoid being active too close to bedtime as it might invigorate you and make it harder to fall asleep.
- **Mindfulness and Relaxation Techniques:** Deep breathing exercises, meditation, or progressive muscle relaxation can reduce anxiety and calm the mind, making it easier to drift into sleep.
- **Limit Naps:** While napping can be beneficial, long or irregular napping can negatively affect your sleep. If you choose to nap, keep it short - between 20-30 minutes.

- **Natural Sleep Aids**: Consider non-prescription sleep aids like melatonin, chamomile tea, or lavender essential oils. Always consult with a healthcare provider before taking any supplements.
- **Stay Away from the Clock:** Staring at a clock when you can't sleep can increase stress. If possible, remove the clock's face from view.
- **Seek Professional Help:** If you've tried multiple methods and still struggle with sleep, consider seeking help from a sleep specialist. Conditions such as sleep apnea, restless legs syndrome, or other sleep disorders might be the cause.

HACK FOUR Routine Check

Alright, let's chat about our lad, Matt, from one of those bustling London universities. If there's anyone who knows about the chaos of city life, juggling lectures, societies, part-time work, and a slice of social life, it's him. But here's the kicker: Matt's got his routine down to an art form. How? Let's break it down.

The Power of The Morning Routine: Before you groan and think of 5 am wake-up calls, that's not Matt's style. He's no early bird. But when he does wake up, the first hour is 'Matt Time'. No phones, no emails. Just him, a hearty breakfast, and a bit of mindfulness meditation to set the tone for the day. Oh, and the most crucial bit? A glass of water to kickstart his system. It's simple but sets a positive trajectory for the day.

Time Blocks, Not To-Do Lists: Matt doesn't work with endless to-do lists. They're a one-way ticket to Overwhelm City. Instead, he uses time blocks. Lectures from 10-12, gym at 3, study session from 4-6, and maybe a cheeky pint at the local at 8. By allocating specific blocks, he ensures he's not biting off more than he can chew. Plus, seeing free blocks motivates him to use them wisely – be it for relaxation or catching up on some reading.

Breaks Are Not Lazy: One of Matt's golden rules? Never study for more than an hour straight. After 60 minutes, he takes a 10-minute break. A walk, a stretch, or even a quick snack. It might seem counterproductive, but these little breaks prevent burnout and keep his mind sharp.

Night Owl Tactics: As said, Matt isn't big on early mornings. But he's got his nighttime routine on lock. An hour before bed, out go the electronics. In their place? A good old-fashioned book. Not a thriller or a mystery, but something light to wind down. He also swears by a quick jotting down of the next day's main tasks. It offloads worries and clears his mind for a restful sleep.

Matt's mantra? "Routine is freedom." By having a structured day, he's not restricting himself; he's creating pockets of free time, ensuring he's on top of his commitments, and most importantly, allowing himself to enjoy the university experience fully. Take a page out of his book, or better yet, craft your own routine. Your future self will thank you.

HACK FIVE

Holistic Health Hubs – Making the Most of Campus Resources

We all know uni life can be a whirlwind of emotions. From the euphoria of acing an exam to the stress of assignment deadlines, it's a rollercoaster. But here's the thing – universities aren't just academic hubs; they're full-fledged ecosystems designed with student wellbeing at the core.

- **Counselling Services:** Feel like things are getting a bit too much? Whether it's academic stress, personal issues, or even the dreaded homesickness, campuses usually have professional counselling services on hand. Confidential and often free, they offer a safe space for students to voice their concerns and get the support they need. Plus, they're geared towards addressing the unique challenges faced by students. It's okay to seek help; it's a sign of strength, not weakness.

- **Health Centers:** From that pesky cold going around to more pressing health issues, campus health centers are your go-to. They're typically staffed with knowledgeable professionals familiar with common student ailments. Plus, they can often provide discounted or even free services, from general check-ups to vaccinations. Don't neglect your physical health; it's the foundation of your mental and emotional wellbeing.

- **Wellness Programs:** Looking to dabble in yoga? Or maybe you fancy a mindfulness workshop? Many universities offer wellness programs geared towards holistic health. They understand that a healthy student is not just about good grades but about overall wellbeing. From fitness classes to meditation sessions, there's likely something on offer to pique your interest.

- **Peer Support Groups:** Sometimes, talking to someone who's in the same boat can be incredibly therapeutic. Many campuses have peer support groups where students can share their experiences, challenges, and triumphs. It's a reminder that you're not alone, and there's a whole community out there to lean on.

- **Mental Health Initiatives:** With rising awareness about the importance of mental health, many universities have started initiatives to support students. This can range from workshops on stress management to campaigns promoting mental health awareness.

Tapping into these resources can be a game-changer. They're right there, often a short walk from your dorm or lecture hall, waiting to be used. Remember, taking care of your health – mind, body, and soul – isn't a luxury; it's a necessity. So, next time you feel out of sorts or just need a bit of TLC, don't hesitate to reach out. Your university's got your back.

08 Chapter 8 - Dormitory/Shared Living

Ah, the joys of shared living! While movies might show you epic dorm parties and endless late-night chats, there's also the other side. You know, like the unrinsed dishes that sit for a fortnight or the impromptu 4 am EDM sessions your roommate decides to hold. Love it or hate it, communal living is a rite of passage. But fret not, we've got some hacks to make this experience more harmonious than horrifying.

HACK ONE
The Sacred Communal Code – Smoothing Out the Shared Living Wrinkles

Alright, let's face it: coexisting in a shared space can be a bit like navigating uncharted waters. Some folks have this uncanny ability to glide seamlessly into a harmonious living situation – like ducks to water. But, for many, the transition isn't always so graceful. If you feel like you're wading through murky waters with your flatmates, then this hack's for you.

1. Group Meeting: The Icebreaker Session
Initiating the first group meeting might feel a bit formal, but it's a game-changer. This isn't about laying down the law or drafting a constitution. Instead, it's an opportunity to get to know each other's quirks, habits, and boundaries. Use this as a chance to find common ground and to set some basic house principles. And hey, throwing in some snacks never hurts to sweeten the deal.

2. Setting Mutual Boundaries:

Harmony Over Rules .Yes, rules sound stringent, but think of them more as mutual boundaries – guidelines that ensure everyone feels respected and at home. It could be simple things: if someone's got a morning exam, maybe the living room stays quiet the night before. Or perhaps there's a communal agreement that whoever didn't cook, does the dishes. These aren't strict regulations but shared understandings that make cohabitation smoother.

3. Rota System: Sharing the Load

When chores get divvied up, it's all about fairness. Maybe you hate vacuuming but don't mind doing the dishes. Perhaps Sarah can't stand cleaning the bathroom but is okay with taking out the trash. Drafting a rota is about playing to each person's strengths and preferences. It's not about rigidly following a timetable, but ensuring that no one feels overwhelmed or taken advantage of.

4. The Communal Kitty: Sharing Costs Without Drama

Money squabbles can turn a happy house sour faster than milk left out of the fridge. A shared pot of funds – the 'Communal Kitty' – can be a lifesaver. Everyone chips in a set amount regularly. This fund is used for shared expenses like cleaning supplies, shared groceries, or that monthly Netflix subscription everyone enjoys. It eliminates those awkward "you owe me" chats and ensures transparency in expenses.

Navigating shared living isn't about setting a rigid framework. Instead, it's about creating a flexible environment where everyone feels heard and respected. The Sacred Communal Code isn't a set of edicts carved in stone. It's a living document, something that can be revisited and tweaked as the living situation evolves. By addressing potential issues head-on and communicating openly, you're setting the stage for a harmonious living experience

HACK TWO

Trust, But Verify – Your Visual Diary Against Housing Woes

Ah, student accommodations. As fun and liberating as they can be, there's that niggling bit of advice you've probably seen all over student forums, or, more recently, from TikTok pros like @rachellord22: Document everything. This isn't about being paranoid; it's about being prepared.

Let's spin you the tale of Jodi, a first-year student at the University of Leeds. Overflowing with excitement, Jodi moved into her student housing, her first real taste of independence. She loved her room, even with its slightly chipped paint and the unassuming little stain on the carpet. To her, these imperfections added character. Fast forward to the end of the year, and she's slapped with unexpected charges for "damages". The little carpet stain? That'd be £50. The chipped paint? Another £30. She was flabbergasted. If only she'd taken photos as evidence when moving in!

Many housing companies, unfortunately, can be a bit... slippery. Not all, of course, but enough to warrant caution. Some might rely on the naivety of freshers, pinning existing damages on them. After all, what fresher has the foresight to document every little nick and scratch?

Here's your action plan, inspired by seasoned students and the wise words of @rachellord22:

- Move-In Day Inspection: On day one, be it a dorm or a shared house, whip out your phone. Take pictures and even videos of every nook and cranny. Those images will capture the exact state of your accommodation.
- Cloud Storage: Backup these photos and videos on cloud storage. Google Drive, Dropbox, or even iCloud. This ensures they're safe and time-stamped, just in case your phone decides to conk out mid-year.
- End of Tenancy: Before moving out, do a final tour and repeat the documentation process. This way, you have a before-and-after snapshot of your living space.
- Communicate with Housing Providers: Be proactive. Share the photos with your housing provider or landlord when moving in, clearly highlighting any existing damages. This can prevent potential disputes down the line.

Takeaway: While we wish every housing provider was the epitome of reliability and integrity, some just aren't. Like Jodi learned the hard way, a few minutes of diligence can save you not just money, but also the headache of unwarranted disputes. Your future self will thank you, and your bank account will too.

HACK THREE
Know Thy Neighbourhood – Your Explorer's Blueprint

Whether you've just moved into a new city for uni or have just shifted dorms, the allure of a new space is undeniable. But, what's even better than that fresh-room feeling? Truly getting to know the beating heart of your area.

Meet Tara, fresh into her first year at University of Manchester. After moving into her accommodation, the first thing she did wasn't decorating her room. No, she strapped on her sneakers and decided to play Dora the Explorer. Why? Because understanding your surroundings doesn't just make life more convenient, it also enriches your university experience.

Here's how to do the Tara way:

- **Essentials First:** Map out the essentials – the nearest grocery shops, pharmacies, post office, and laundromat. Knowing you can grab a pint of milk or some paracetamol within a 5-minute walk is immensely reassuring.
- **The Fun Hunt:** Now for the fun stuff. Coffee shops, pubs, restaurants, shopping centres, and more. Discovering where the best flat white is or which pub has the best student deals can be a game changer.
- **Fitness and Well-being:** If you're the type to enjoy a good workout, find the closest gyms. Alternatively, look for parks or open spaces for a refreshing morning jog or a tranquil evening walk.
- **Cultural Hotspots:** Museums, art galleries, libraries, theatres. Even if they're not your usual haunts, give them a try. You might just discover a newfound love for Shakespearean plays or post-modern art!
- **Safety First:** Familiarise yourself with the streets. Know which areas are bustling and well-lit at night, and which might be better avoided after dark.
- **Make a Day of It:** The whole process doesn't have to be utilitarian. Call up a mate or two, or team up with new roommates and make a day of it. Wander around, maybe grab a bite, and you're not just discovering the area but also building connections.

Remember: Your uni years are not just about what's within the campus walls but also what lies beyond. The neighbourhood can, and will, shape a significant part of your student life. Knowing where to grab a late-night snack or where to find a quiet reading spot can make your experience richer and more varied. So, channel your inner explorer and embark on the grand adventure right outside your door!

HACK FOUR

The Pre-Unpack Clean – Because Fresh Starts Need Fresh Spaces

Imagine this: You've just carted up a bazillion boxes, bags, and what-nots to your dorm. Everything's in a chaotic pile. You're tempted to just start unpacking, setting things up, and making the space yours. But, hold on a tick! Before you start that chaotic symphony of unzipping and box-opening, there's one crucial step many overlook – a deep clean.

Here's the deal: Even if the housing team gives you a well-intentioned thumbs up, asserting they've cleaned the place, take it with a pinch of salt. They might have given it a once-over, but think about it. The previous occupant could have been someone with a mouldy sandwich collection. Or someone who thought that kitchen counters were self-cleaning. Gross, right? So, how should you go about it?

- **Cleaning Supplies Ready:** Arm yourself with disinfecting wipes, multi-surface cleaners, a scrub, gloves, and garbage bags. They'll be your trusty comrades in this mission.
- **The Big Sweep:** Before you start scrubbing, sweep or vacuum the floor to rid it of dust and other debris.
- **Surface Attack:** Wipe down all surfaces – from your study desk to kitchen counters. Pay special attention to door handles and light switches; they're often missed but are hotspots for germs.
- **Bathroom Deep Dive:** If you have an en-suite, make sure to give the bathroom a thorough clean. This includes the toilet, sink, mirrors, and especially the shower. Because, trust us, you don't want to know what hair horrors could be lurking there.
- **Kitchen Chronicles:** If it's a shared kitchen, rally your roomies for a joint cleaning session. Ensure the fridge, microwave, stove, and oven are spotless. Remember, a clean kitchen is the first step to avoiding those pesky pests!
- **Air It Out:** Once done, open the windows wide and let fresh air sweep through your now-spick-and-span space.
- **Freshen Up:** Consider adding some fragrant touches to your room. Whether it's a pleasant room spray, scented candles (if allowed), or even some fresh flowers, they can make your space feel all the more welcoming and homey.

Now, with your room fresh and gleaming, you're truly ready to unpack and nestle in. Starting off with a clean slate – or in this case, a clean room – sets a positive tone for the academic year ahead. It's not just about hygiene; it's about creating a space where you'll feel comfortable, focused, and at peace.

HACK FIVE

Cultivate Genuine Connections – Beyond the Initial Chat

Selecting your uni accommodation is akin to picking your uni experience. So, let's dive into a step-by-step guide to ensure your choice isn't just about four walls, but an enriching chapter of your life:

1. Catered vs. Non-Catered: The Culinary Conundrum.
- How to Decide?
  - Sample the Offerings: Campus tours often include meals. Don't just eat; evaluate.
  - Get the Gossip: Connect with current students on platforms like The Student Room or UniBuddy to ask about the food's quality and variety.
  - Self-Assess: Are you a budding chef or more of a cereal-for-dinner individual? Non-catered offers freedom but also demands responsibility.

2. Bathroom Chronicles: En-suite vs. Shared:
- How to Decide?
  - Analyse Your Routine: If you're always dashing about in the mornings, an en-suite might be worth the investment.
  - Get the Ratio: Ask about the number of students per shared bathroom. Fewer people to a bathroom might make sharing more bearable.

3. The Money Matters: Budgeting:
- How to Decide?
  - Break It Down: List all your potential expenses and see how much you can allocate to rent. Remember, it's not just about the monthly rate; consider utility bills if they aren't included.
  - Do Some Digging: Platforms like Save the Student provide insights into average rent rates in various cities.

4. Pinpointing the Perfect Location:

- Visualise Your Day: List places you'll frequent (library, favourite cafe, gym). Use Google Maps to see which accommodations are centrally located.
- Think Transport: If you're a tad further out, check public transport links and costs. Sometimes a slightly more expensive place closer to the action can save money in the long run.

5. Vibe and Tribe: Sociable or Sanctuary?

- Personality Check: Are you looking for a lively spot or a peaceful haven? Some accommodations are known for their social vibes, while others are quieter.
- Chat with Predecessors: Current or past residents will give you the lowdown on the true atmosphere of the place.

6. Extra Amenities: Beyond the Basics.

- Prioritise: Do you need a study room? Bike storage? Gym? Rank your needs.
- Double-Check: Don't take adverts at face value. Confirm with the accommodation office or current residents.

7. Security Matters: Peace of Mind.

- Scope It Out: Ask about security measures – from CCTV to entry systems.
- Local Knowledge: Some student forums discuss safer areas in cities. Worth a peek!

8. Know Your Contract: Before Signing on the Dotted Line.

- Decode the Details: Know the contract length, terms for breaking it, and bill inclusions.
- Get a Second Opinion: Have someone seasoned (like an older student or a guardian) review it.

9. Physical Visits: The Real Litmus Test.

- o Go In-Person: Photos can be deceiving. If possible, visit in person.
- o Virtual Tours: Can't visit? Many accommodations offer virtual tours. Still better than just photos!

The essence? Don't rush. Take your time, do your research, and trust your instincts. Your ideal uni home is out there!

And there we have it, the end of this guidebook, but the start of something far bigger - your own uni adventure. It's bound to be a blend of whirlwind excitement, inevitable challenges, late-night laughter, and some last-minute cramming. But armed with these hacks, you're more than ready.

Remember, these tips are tools, not rules. Life isn't an instruction manual, and neither is university. Sometimes, the unexpected detours - the unplanned nights out, the surprise friendships, the unexpected epiphanies at 3 am - end up being the most memorable. So, use these hacks as they suit you. If they help, brilliant. If not, ditch them. Your journey is uniquely yours, after all.

Above all, soak it all in. These days will fly by faster than you think. University is not just about degrees and dorm rooms; it's about discovery, growth, and memories that'll last a lifetime.

So, here's wishing you all the luck and laughter in the world. May your uni days be as legendary as you hope for and even more. Dive in, explore, learn, and most importantly, enjoy every single moment.

Cheers to the journey ahead!